CHARLES DARWIN

THE CHELSEA HOUSE LIBRARY OF BIOGRAPHY

CHARLES DARWIN

DON NARDO

Chelsea House Publishers

New York • Philadelphia

CHELSEA HOUSE PUBLISHERS

Editorial Director   Richard Rennert
Executive Managing Editor   Karyn Gullen Browne
Executive Editor   Sean Dolan
Copy Chief   Philip Koslow
Picture Editor   Adrian Allen
Art Director   Nora Wertz
Manufacturing Director   Gerald Levine
Systems Manager   Lindsey Ottman
Production Coordinator   Marie Claire Cebrián-Ume

The Chelsea House Library of Biography
Senior Editor   Kathy Kuhtz

Staff for **CHARLES DARWIN**
Copy Editor   Danielle Janusz
Editorial Assistant   Laura Petermann
Picture Researcher   Pat Burns
Series Designer   Basia Niemczyc
Cover Illustration   Michael Garland

Printed and bound in Mexico.

First Printing

1   3   5   7   9   8   6   4   2

Library of Congress Cataloging-in-Publication Data

Nardo, Don, 1947–
Charles Darwin/Don Nardo.
p. cm.—(The Chelsea House library of biography)
Includes bibliographical references (P.) and index.
Summary: Focuses on Darwin's development of his idea of natural selection, his voyage to the Galapagos Islands, and the publication and defense of his works.
ISBN 0-7910-1729-X
        0-7910-1730-3 (pbk.)
1. Darwin, Charles 1809–1882—Juvenile literature. 2. Naturalists—England—Biography—Juvenile literature. [1. Darwin, Charles, 1809–1882. 2. Naturalists. 3. Evolution.] I. Title. II. Series.
QH31.D2N35 1993   92-24365
575'.0092—dc20   CIP
[B]   AC

Contents

THE CHELSEA HOUSE LIBRARY OF BIOGRAPHY

Barbara Bush

John C. Calhoun

Clarence Darrow

Charles Darwin

Anne Frank

William Lloyd Garrison

Martha Graham

J. Edgar Hoover

Saddam Hussein

Jesse James

Rose Kennedy

John Lennon

Jack London

Horace Mann

Muhammad

Edward R. Murrow

William Penn

Edgar Allan Poe

Norman Schwarzkopf

Joseph Smith

Sam Walton

Frank Lloyd Wright

Boris Yeltsin

Brigham Young

Other titles in the series are forthcoming.

Introduction

Learning from Biographies

Vito Perrone

The oldest narratives that exist are biographical. Much of what we know, for example, about the Pharaohs of ancient Egypt, the builders of Babylon, the philosophers of Greece, the rulers of Rome, the many biblical and religious leaders who provide the base for contemporary spiritual beliefs, has come to us through biographies—the stories of their lives. Although an oral tradition was long the mainstay of historically important biographical accounts, the oral stories making up this tradition became by the 1st century A.D. central elements of a growing written literature.

In the 1st century A.D., biography assumed a more formal quality through the work of such writers as Plutarch, who left us more than 500 biographies of political and intellectual leaders of Rome and Greece. This tradition of focusing on great personages lasted well into the 20th century and is seen as an important means of understanding the history of various times and places. We learn much, for example, from Plutarch's writing about the collapse of the Greek city-states and about the struggles in Rome over the justice and the constitutionality of a world empire. We also gain considerable understanding of the definitions of morality and civic virtue and how various common men and women lived out their daily existence.

Not surprisingly, the earliest American writing, beginning in the 17th century, was heavily biographical. Those Europeans who came to America were dedicated to recording their experience, especially the struggles they faced in building what they determined to be a new culture. John Norton's *Life and Death of John Cotton*, printed in 1630, typifies these early works. Later biographers often tackled more ambitious projects. Cotton Mather's *Magnalia Christi Americana*, published in 1702, accounted for the lives of more than 70 ministers and political leaders. In addition, a biographical literature around the theme of Indian captivity had considerable popularity. Soon after the American Revolution and the organization of the United States of America, Americans were treated to a large outpouring of biographies about such figures as Benjamin Franklin, George Washington, Thomas Jefferson, and Aaron Burr, among others. These particular works served to build a strong sense of national identity.

Among the diverse forms of historical literature, biographies have been over many centuries the most popular. And in recent years interest in biography has grown even greater, as biography has gone beyond prominent government figures, military leaders, giants of business, industry, literature, and the arts. Today we are treated increasingly to biographies of more common people who have inspired others by their particular acts of courage, by their positions on important social and political issues, or by their dedicated lives as teachers, town physicians, mothers, and fathers. Through this broader biographical literature, much of which is featured in the CHELSEA HOUSE LIBRARY OF BIOGRAPHY, our historical understandings can be enriched greatly.

What makes biography so compelling? Most important, biography is a human story. In this regard, it makes of history something personal, a narrative with which we can make an intimate connection. Biographers typically ask us as readers to accompany them on a journey through the life of another person, to see some part of the world through another's eyes. We can, as a result, come to understand what it is like to live the life of a slave, a farmer, a textile worker, an engineer, a poet, a president—in a sense, to walk in another's shoes. Such experience can be personally invaluable. We cannot ask for a better entry into historical studies.

Although our personal lives are likely not as full as those we are reading about, there will be in most biographical accounts many common experiences. As with the principal character of any biography, we are also faced with numerous decisions, large and small. In the midst of living our lives we are not usually able to comprehend easily the significance of our daily decisions or grasp easily their many possible consequences, but we can gain important insights into them by seeing the decisions made by others play themselves out. We can learn from others.

Because biography is a personal story, it is almost always full of surprises. So often, the personal lives of individuals we come across historically are out of view, their public personas masking who they are. It is through biography that we gain access to their private lives, to the acts that define who they are and what they truly care about. We see their struggles within the possibilities and limitations of life, gaining insight into their beliefs, the ways they survived hardships, what motivated them, and what discouraged them. In the process we can come to understand better our own struggles.

As you read this biography, try to place yourself within the subject's world. See the events as that person sees them. Try to understand why the individual made particular decisions and not others. Ask yourself if you would have chosen differently. What are the values or beliefs that guide the subject's actions? How are those values or beliefs similar to yours? How are they different from yours? Above all, remember: You are engaging in an important historical inquiry as you read a biography, but you are also reading a literature that raises important personal questions for you to consider.

Twenty-six-year-old Charles Robert Darwin sailed aboard the HMS Beagle *as the ship's naturalist, studying the geology, plants, and animals of each of the lands he visited in his five-year around-the-world voyage of exploration.*

1

The Mysterious Islands

THE YOUNG MAN AND THE HIDEOUS BEAST eyed each other cautiously. Twenty-six-year-old Charles Darwin stood only a few feet away from the four-foot-long lizard, which staunchly guarded the entrance to its underground burrow. The creature was covered with scales, had a long ridge of sharp spines along its back, and possessed huge, menacing-looking claws. Its long, moist tongue flickered in Darwin's direction. Out of the corner of his eye, the young man could see other giant lizards, some watching him, others climbing high into cactus trees and feeding on the succulent branches.

Suddenly, the lizard nearest Darwin turned and began climbing into the burrow. Acting quickly, he lunged forward, grabbed the lizard's receding tail, and yanked the creature back out into the daylight. Expecting an attack, Darwin immediately took several steps backward. But the lizard only stared at him with what appeared to be a look of surprise, then turned and retreated once again into the earth. In other

*Darwin encountered land iguana (*Amblyrynchus demarlii), *such as the specimen illustrated here, during his exploration of the Galápagos Islands and confirmed that these ferocious-looking beasts were, indeed, harmless. In his journal, Darwin described the lizards as "essentially mild and torpid monsters."*

similar experiments, Darwin verified that these fierce-looking beasts were not particularly dangerous. Later in the day, he made an entry in his notebook describing these land iguana, or lizards, as "essentially mild and torpid [sluggish] monsters."

As the sun dipped low in the sky on that hot September day in 1835, Darwin turned away from the iguana colony and made his way toward the beach. There, four other men from the British ship the HMS *Beagle* had just finished setting up a large tent and were already preparing supper. Early that morning, a dinghy from the ship had transported the five men to the shore of James Island, and Captain Robert FitzRoy had promised to pick them up in a week. That would give Darwin enough time to explore the place and observe the local animals. As the ship's naturalist, it was his job to study the geology, the plants, and the animals of each of the lands the ship visited in its around-the-world voyage of mapping and discovery.

Since leaving England on December 27, 1831, more than three years before, the *Beagle* had already traveled extensively along the eastern coast of South America. In addition to visiting the bustling and colorful city of Buenos Aires, the ship had navigated Argentine rivers to explore farther inland. During his inland explorations Darwin had enjoyed meeting and riding with Argentine cowboys, called gauchos, who had shown him rare ostriches and other exotic animals. The *Beagle* also visited the islands at the tip of South America that Magellan had discovered three centuries before. From there, the ship had sailed northward into the Pacific Ocean and landed in Chile, where Darwin experienced the awesome power of a killer earthquake. Next, the *Beagle* and its passengers had reached the desolate and very mysterious Galápagos Islands, located directly along the equator about 500 miles off the western coast of South America. At the time, Ecuador claimed ownership of this 100-mile-long island chain.

Way off the main marine routes, the Galápagos were isolated and seldom visited, although a few whalers and other ships occasionally stopped to rest and hunt for food. The islands were mostly arid and volcanic, with few trees and little vegetation, which made them practically uninhabitable. In the journal he kept during the voyage, Darwin wrote:

> Nothing could be less inviting than the first appearance [of the islands]. A broken field of black basaltic lava is every where covered by a stunted brushwood, which shows little signs of life. The dry and parched surface, having been heated by the noonday sun, gave the air a close and sultry feeling, like that from a stove: We fancied even the bushes smelt unpleasantly.

But, despite their bleakness, the islands did draw a few infrequent sightseers, such as the crew of the *Beagle*. This was because the Galápagos were strange, primitive islands, inhabited by animals seen nowhere else in the world. For a naturalist like Darwin, the Galápagos constituted a wonderland of sights and sounds reminiscent of a prehistoric landscape. In addition to the huge lizards, there were many gigantic tortoises, bright red crabs, large seals, exotic birds, and other unusual animals roaming the islands. To Darwin, it seemed as though he was witness to the way the earth appeared when the very first primitive creatures crawled across the land. "Here," he wrote in his notes, "both in space and time, we seem to be brought somewhat near to that great fact—that mystery of mysteries—the first appearance of new beings on this earth."

How *had* animals and people first appeared on earth? This question had occupied Darwin's thoughts more and more frequently as the *Beagle*'s voyage progressed. Ever since childhood, he had accepted the traditional religious explanation—that God had created the earth and all living things in the space of just a few days. Since the time of the Creation, according to this view, plants and animals had kept the same forms. They did not evolve, or change, over the course of time.

But Darwin had begun to doubt this explanation, for during the *Beagle*'s travels, he had seen on a number of occasions different forms of the same animal living very near each other. For instance, in Argentina, within an area of only a few hundred square miles, he had observed two kinds of ostrich. They were obviously related but showed definitely discernible physical differences. Why, Darwin asked himself, would God create two so similar types of ostrich and place them in the same region? This did not seem logical to the young naturalist. He did not want to question the Creator's logic, but his instincts told him that some grand and powerful natural principle or force had made these animals different. Would he find similar examples of variations in species in the Galápagos? Possessed with a scientist's three most important tools— acute powers of observation, a sharp, logical mind, and a driving curiosity—he set about studying the animals of the Galápagos in more detail.

Darwin found the creatures of these islands both strange and fascinating. One day on James Island, he and one of his companions found two giant tortoises feeding on some large cacti. The creatures were deaf and did not notice the men until they walked directly into the tortoises' line of

Giant tortoises were among the many strange and exotic reptiles that Darwin observed roaming the Galápagos Islands. Darwin calculated that each tortoise, whose shell measured about 8 feet in circumference, weighed at least 500 pounds and walked a distance of about 60 yards in 10 minutes.

sight. Upon seeing the humans, the tortoises hissed loudly and drew their heads into their shells. Darwin marveled at the great size of the animals. He estimated that their shells were more than four feet long and about eight feet in circumference. And each tortoise weighed at least 500 pounds. The two men tried to lift the creatures and turn them over but found this impossible. Then, they decided to ride the tortoises, which, apparently unhindered by the weight of the men, kept on walking. Darwin estimated that the beasts covered about 60 yards in 10 minutes, a rate of about 360 yards an hour. The naturalist made an entry in his notebook calculating that a giant tortoise could travel about four miles a day, "allowing a little time for it to eat on the road."

Later in the day, the two men found a spring of water at which two lines of giant tortoises had formed. The members of one line were moving away from the spring, obviously having just finished filling themselves up with water. The other tortoises, their necks outstretched, were heading directly toward the spring. "Quite regardless of any spectator, the tortoise buries his head in the water above his eyes, and greedily swallows great mouthfuls, at the rate of about ten in a minute," wrote Darwin. The men learned that the creatures drank in this fashion only about once a month.

Darwin noticed empty tortoise shells all over the island. Some of these had been discarded by whalers and other sailors who sometimes came ashore and killed the huge creatures for food. The rest of the shells were probably the remains of tortoises that had died and been picked clean by scavengers. Darwin and his companions cooked a tortoise themselves and found that the meat was delicious, especially when the animal was roasted in the shell.

The shells proved to be more than a mere curiosity to Darwin. They showed him that the same natural principle that had produced the two varieties of ostrich was also at work in the Galápagos. After studying tortoise shells from several Galápagos islands, he could see plainly that slightly different varieties of tortoise inhabited different islands. An Englishman in Ecuador had earlier told him that the shells were so distinct that Ecuadorians "could with certainty tell from which [Galápagos] island any one was brought." Darwin had now verified this claim. He was intrigued, writing in his journal:

> I never dreamed that islands, about fifty or sixty miles apart, and most of them in sight of each other, formed of precisely the same rocks, placed under a quite similar climate, rising to a near equal height, would have been differently tenanted [inhabited].

Darwin also found similar unexplained differences in many species of birds inhabiting the Galápagos. He delighted in studying these birds, which he found colorful and "very curious." He counted 26 species of land birds on James Island alone. Because most of the birds had never seen humans before, they were unafraid of Darwin and his associates. Apparently, the birds thought that people were as harmless to them as the tortoises, lizards, and other local animals. It was not unusual, for example, to see an iguana and a bird casually eating from opposite ends of one small piece of cactus. When Darwin walked through bushes in which birds were perched, the birds sat unmoving and observed him casually. When he held a pitcher of water in his hand, a mockingbird flew down, landed on the rim of the container and took a drink. He found it easy to knock a bird off a branch with a leisurely swat of his hat. Clearly, these birds were very different than any he had seen before.

The observation that most interested Darwin about the Galápagos birds was that, like the tortoises, a single species displayed noticeable differences from island to island. For example, the finches on each island had their own uniquely-shaped beaks. The finches on one island had thick, strong beaks used to crack nuts and seeds,

whereas those of a neighboring island had smaller beaks better suited to feeding on fruits and flowers. Another type of finch possessed a beak designed to catch insects and still another used its beak like that of a woodpecker to extract insect larvae from tree bark. Why, Darwin wondered, were there so many different types of finch on neighboring islands having the same general climate and terrain? And why were all of these finches similar to, yet distinctly different from, the finches that lived on the distant mainland of South America?

An explanation, still vague and unsupported, but compelling in its beauty and simplicity, began to form in Darwin's mind. He did not conceive the idea all at once, but instead pieced it together gradually during the return voyage and in the months following his return to England. Later, he wrote the now famous sentence summing up the origin of this idea: "Seeing this gradation [succession of differences] and diversity of structure in one small, intimately related group of birds, one might really fancy that from an original paucity [lack] of birds in this archipelago [island chain], one species had been taken and modified for different ends."

By saying that one kind of bird had been modified, Darwin was suggesting that a species might be capable of changing its physical form on its own. This was not a new idea. Other researchers, including French scientist Jean-Baptiste de Lamarck (1744–1829), had earlier suggested that animal and plant species might undergo change, or "transmutation," over the course of time. Darwin's own grandfather, Erasmus Darwin, had proposed a similar theory. But the scientists of Darwin's day had rejected such ideas and strongly supported the biblical explanation of the Creation. There was, they insisted, no evidence whatsoever for evolutionary change.

Yet here, on a chain of remote and mysterious Pacific islands, Darwin had found such evidence. Perhaps, he thought, the Galápagos had once been barren of life.

Opposite:
Darwin based much of his theory of evolution on the finches, now known as Darwin's finches, that he studied on the Galápagos Islands. Darwin noticed that the finches on each island had their own uniquely shaped beaks even though they lived on neighboring islands that had the same general climate and terrain.

Over the course of time, finches from the mainland might occasionally have been caught in wind currents and have flown to the islands. There, the birds found environmental conditions unlike those they were used to. Different foods were available to them and they had to adjust to unfamiliar habitats. Eventually, Darwin theorized, through countless successive generations, the finches changed, a little at a time, to adjust to their new environments. Because conditions differed slightly from island to island, the birds of each island adapted in their own unique way.

Darwin thought that the same argument might be applied to the tortoises. The first tortoises, he proposed, might have arrived on the Galápagos shores after a long sea journey. In time, like the birds, they too would have adjusted to their isolated and very distinct environment by undergoing physical changes. Presumably, these changes would better enable the animals to continue to survive and reproduce. But what could be causing these changes? Darwin could think of no logical way to explain how a species could change in form. Yet he could not ignore the overwhelming evidence of changes in species that he had uncovered in the Galápagos Islands.

Darwin realized that his idea had momentous and controversial implications. If such physical changes in species had actually occurred in the recent past on the Galápagos, presumably they had occurred throughout history all around the world. Given enough time, such small changes in one kind of animal might add up and the end result could be a completely new variety of that animal. This, thought Darwin, might be how new species periodically come into existence. This idea greatly disturbed Darwin. If the living things of the world had evolved through some natural process, it would mean that God had not created them all at once as described in the Bible. Thus, perhaps this and other biblical stories were not literally true, as most people believed. Darwin knew that many people would find this upsetting, if not unbelievable.

With the *Beagle* moving swiftly from island to island, Darwin usually had only a few days in which to study the animals and plants of any one island. Therefore, exploring, observing, and organizing specimens consumed most of his waking hours and he had little time to think about and develop his idea of evolving species. Late in 1835, the *Beagle* departed the Galápagos and Darwin bade farewell to these strange, lonely islands and the collection of fascinating, often bizarre creatures that inhabited them. In the following months, he studied his journal notes and specimens and slowly began to construct a theory that would explain the phenomena he had observed. At the time, he had little notion that this theory would someday profoundly reshape scientific thought and forever change the way people viewed the natural world and their place within it.

Charles Darwin was seven years old when he and his sister Catherine posed for this painting in 1816. Charles, the fifth of six children, had parents who instilled a love of learning in their children, but in spite of his family's faith in education, young Charles was not a zealous student.

2

Searching for Himself

ON FEBRUARY 12, 1809, in the town of Shrewsbury, near the border between England and Wales, Robert and Susannah Darwin had a son, whom they named Charles Robert. He was the fifth of their six children, four of whom were girls. At the time, Shrewsbury was a busy market town built on a series of low hills overlooking the Severn River. The rich farmlands of Shropshire, some of the most bountiful and attractive countryside in the British Isles, surrounded the town.

Robert Darwin was the most respected and well-to-do doctor in Shrewsbury. He was known not only for his healing skills but also for his keen sense of humor and imposing physical presence. Six feet two inches tall and weighing 330 pounds, he commanded attention, and young Charles was in awe of him. Seldom did the boy disagree with his father, and when he did, he dared not do so to the man's face.

The success Robert Darwin achieved as a physician enabled his family to live a comfortable life as part of England's growing upper middle class. The house Charles grew up in was large and each

Robert Waring Darwin, Charles's father, was the most respected doctor in Shrewsbury and became known for his clever sense of humor and imposing physical presence—even his son Charles was in awe of him. As Charles grew older and spent his free time hunting, riding, and taking nature walks, the elder Darwin often showed his disapproval of his son's impractical pursuits.

child had his or her own room. There were lovely, well-kept gardens surrounding the house and several servants to do the chores and wait on the family. Thus, unlike so many other children in Shropshire, who had to help their struggling parents by working in the fields, the Darwin children enjoyed a life of luxury with plenty of time for play. There was also ample time for reading and learning. Because Charles's parents were well-educated, they encouraged learning and made sure that there were many books available for the children's use.

In fact, the pursuit of knowledge was something of a tradition among Charles's relatives. Susannah's father was Josiah Wedgwood, the renowned maker of fine pottery. A philanthropist, Wedgwood contributed time and money to worthy causes, especially education, and instilled a love of learning in all of his children, including Charles's mother. And the boy's paternal grandfather, Erasmus Darwin, had been a well-known physician and scholar. Besides being offered and subsequently refusing the position of physician to King George III, Erasmus Darwin had written a number of widely read volumes about nature.

One particular idea put forward by Erasmus Darwin aroused controversy in learned circles in the late 1770s. He suggested that each kind of animal and plant had descended from an original parent animal that had lived several million years before. The different living species, said Darwin, not only had been reproducing for a long time but also had a tendency to "improve" themselves a little at a time. Most of Darwin's colleagues thought this concept was wrong for two reasons. First, nearly everyone at the time assumed that the earth was only a few thousand years old. Religious scholars had counted backwards the generations listed in the Bible, the contents of which were looked upon as literally factual, and dated the creation of the universe at about 6,000 years before the present day.

The second reason that scholars rejected Erasmus Darwin's idea was that it went against the established biblical doctrine that God had created all living things in their present forms. Animals and plants, insisted the religious argument, had remained unchanged ever since. Many people criticized Darwin sharply for suggesting the Bible might be in error and they called him an atheist, an extremely derogatory term at the time. Young Charles Darwin was aware of his grandfather's idea about the descent of animals and plants. But the concept made little impression on the boy, who, devoutly religious, automatically accepted the popular biblical view of the Creation. Later, as an adult, Darwin would drastically reconsider the notions of an ancient earth and evolving life.

Despite his family's emphasis on learning and education, young Charles Darwin was not an avid or remarkable student. In 1818, at the age of nine, his father—his mother had died the year before—enrolled him in Shrewsbury School, about a mile from their home. There, under headmaster Dr. Samuel Butler, Darwin studied Latin, the

Darwin spent his childhood in Shrewsbury, a market town located amid the rich farmlands and rolling hills of Shropshire, a county in western England near the border of Wales.

Susannah Wedgwood Darwin, the daughter of Josiah Wedgwood, the well-known maker of fine pottery, died when her son Charles was eight years old. One year after his mother's death, Charles was sent to Shrewsbury School to study Latin, history, and the classics— subjects that his father thought were crucial for his education but that Charles found uninteresting.

classics, and history, but found all of these subjects dull. He especially hated memorizing and reciting long tracts of Latin and Greek verse, feeling such rote learning was a waste of his time. He preferred science, especially topics relating to nature. However, at the time, science was not yet systematically taught in the schools. Most headmasters and teachers in England felt that science was useless and maintained that a firm background in the classics was the only necessary training for gentlemen and ladies of the upper classes.

Darwin learned the hard way how much his own headmaster disapproved of science. Darwin's brother, Erasmus, set up a makeshift chemistry lab in the family's toolshed and Darwin enjoyed helping him with various experiments. Darwin spent so much time in the lab that his friends began calling him "Gas," and eventually, Dr. Butler learned what had been distracting the boy from his studies. In front of the entire student body, Butler sternly lectured Darwin about wasting time on such useless pursuits. This embarrassing episode only made the boy dislike school all the more and he consistently received poor grades. Later, Darwin recalled:

> The school as a means of education to me was simply a blank. I learned absolutely nothing except by amusing myself reading and experimenting in chemistry. . . . I was considered by all my masters and by my father as a very ordinary boy, rather below the common standard of intellect.

Chemistry was not Darwin's only out-of-school interest. He liked to take long walks in the fields and forests to observe nature. He also greatly enjoyed shooting birds. "I do not believe," he later wrote, "that anyone could have shown more zeal for the most holy cause than I did for shooting birds." Darwin especially enjoyed hunting near the country estate of his uncle, Josiah Wedgwood, located about 20 miles from Shrewsbury. He recalled being so eager to begin the day's hunt "that I used to place my shooting boots open by my bed-side when I went to bed, so as not to lose half-a-minute in putting them on in the morning." The boy took himself seriously as a hunter. Sometimes he stood in front of a mirror for hours at a time, practicing the most efficient way to swing his gun to his shoulder. As he grew into a teenager, Darwin spent almost all of his free time hunting, riding, taking nature walks, and enjoying similar hobbies.

But Darwin's father did not approve of his son's frivolous lifestyle. The elder Darwin felt the young man was idle and made too little effort to better his mind and plan for the future. "You care for nothing but shooting, dogs, and rat-catching," said Dr. Darwin, "and you will be a disgrace to yourself and all your family." The boy paid little attention to such lectures and continued with his leisure pastimes. Eventually, in 1825, when Darwin was 16, his father finally became fed up, removed him from Dr. Butler's school, and enrolled him in Edinburgh University, where Charles's brother was studying medicine. The young man was forced to study medicine, too, so that he could follow in the footsteps of his father and grandfather before him.

Darwin's studies at the university bored him as much as the ones in Dr. Butler's school. In a letter to one of his sisters, he described one of his courses as being so boring it "cannot be translated into any word expressive of its stupidity." Darwin dreaded going to class and found dissecting animals distasteful in the extreme. Even worse was the spectacle of surgery on a human being. One day he had to attend an operation being performed on a child, who was held down during the procedure, as was the custom, because anesthesia had not yet been used in operating rooms. The child's screams were too much for Darwin and he fled, horrified, from the room.

During his two years in Edinburgh, Darwin did manage to learn some things that would prove useful in his later endeavors. First, he met the French-American naturalist and artist John James Audubon, whose realistic drawings of birds in their natural habitats were soon to become known around the world. Darwin also met a taxidermist, a person who stuffs and mounts birds and animals, who had served on expeditions to the then remote continent of South America. Darwin brought some birds he had recently shot to the man to be stuffed, which, the young man later remembered, "he did excellently: he gave me lessons for payment, and I used often to sit with him, for he was a very pleasant and intelligent man." His experiences with Audubon and the taxidermist expanded Darwin's knowledge of the anatomy and habits of birds. This information would prove invaluable when he himself later visited remote continents and islands.

In 1827, Darwin's father finally realized that his son lacked the interest and motivation necessary to become a doctor. But Dr. Darwin did not want the boy to return home and resume his former life as an "idle sporting man." Consequently, the elder Darwin arranged for his son to study for the ministry at Cambridge University. As a man of the church his son would not make a lot of money, Dr. Darwin admitted, but he would be part of a respectable profession and make something of his life. Darwin spent the next three years at Cambridge and once again found most of his classes boring. For fun, he joined a local student group known as the Glutton Club, whose members met each week to eat, drink, and play cards. He also frequently engaged in riding, shooting, and fox hunting, the very pursuits his father wanted him to abandon.

It was on one of these outings that Darwin's attitude toward hunting suddenly changed. One day the young man shot a bird but could not find the carcass and went home. The next day, he happened upon the bird he had shot. It was still alive and suffering terribly, and Darwin felt great remorse. This experience altered his view of hunting for sport, and he swore thereafter he would kill birds or other animals only for food or for scientific study.

Although his regular courses at school seemed a waste, his personal studies of science continued all through his years at Cambridge. His interest in animals had expanded to include insects and he began collecting different species of beetles. Darwin often wondered why there were so many similar-looking species of beetles inhabiting the same region. Why had God not done the simplest, most expedient thing and made one kind of beetle for each region of the world? Little did he realize that he would soon be considering that same question again in regards to the ostriches and birds of faraway lands. In the meantime, he attempted to collect as many species of beetles as possible. He was so eager, he later recalled, that "one day, on tearing off some old bark, I saw two rare beetles, and seized one

A view from the building where Darwin obtained lodging while studying for the clergy at Christ's College, Cambridge. After Darwin's father realized Charles lacked the incentive to become a doctor, he arranged for him to study religion at Cambridge, where, much to his father's dismay, he often engaged in riding, shooting, and fox hunting.

John Stevens Henslow, a well-known professor of botany at Cambridge, encouraged Darwin's interest in natural science. In fact, it was Henslow who first recognized Darwin's flair for scientific thinking. Darwin frequently accompanied Henslow and his students on their nature walks, and he and Henslow soon became close friends.

in each hand; then I saw a third and new kind, which I could not bear to lose, so that I popped the one which I held in my right hand into my mouth. Alas it ejected some intensely acrid [bitter] fluid, which burnt my tongue so that I was forced to spit the beetle out, which was lost, as well as the third one."

It was also during his stay at Cambridge that Darwin met Reverend John Stevens Henslow, a well-known professor of botany, which is the study of plant life. Often Darwin skipped his own classes to go on nature walks with Henslow and his botany students. Seeing the young man's sincere and intense interest, Henslow did not object. In fact, Darwin accompanied Henslow's classes so often, many students began referring to him as "the man who walks with Henslow." Soon Henslow and Darwin became close friends. Henslow frequently invited Darwin to his house for tea and the two talked about science and how new scientific discoveries were changing the way people viewed the world.

Henslow recognized something in young Charles Darwin that no other adult had observed up to that time: Darwin's flair for scientific thinking and reasoning. The professor urged the young man to give up his other studies and devote his life to science. But Darwin, still influenced by the opinion of his father and many others that science was not a worthy avocation, insisted on keeping his scientific interests a hobby.

Darwin received his bachelor's degree in theology from Cambridge in January 1831. But, because he had begun his first year in the middle of a semester, he still needed a few more credits to satisfy the graduation requirements of the school. So he decided to take a course in geology, the study of the earth and its structure, with Professor Adam Sedgwick. Sedgwick was a brilliant man and an excellent teacher who made Darwin want to learn more about the history of the planet and the nature of the fossil remains beneath the earth's surface. Both Sedgwick and Henslow

strongly urged Darwin to take field trips whenever possible. The best way to learn about the lay of the land and
the living things that inhabit it, they argued, was to study
them firsthand. Following this advice, Darwin accompanied Sedgwick on a field trip to the mountains of
Wales, about 100 miles west of Darwin's hometown of
Shrewsbury.

It was during his studies with Sedgwick that Darwin
read the travel book *A Personal Narrative of Travels to the
Equinoctial Regions of America During the Years 1790–
1804*. The author was the most renowned scientific ex-
plorer of the early 19th century—Baron Alexander von
Humboldt. Darwin became completely fascinated by
Humboldt's descriptions of his adventures in the Canary
Islands, South America, Mexico, and the United States. At
that time, much of these lands remained unexplored and
unnamed and sometimes the members of Humboldt's party
were the first Europeans to see them. Darwin longed to be
a part of such a voyage of discovery, to break new scientific ground and see such wonders for himself.

For Darwin, the following months seemed like an impossible dream come true. Upon returning home from his
trip to Wales, he found a letter waiting from Henslow. The
Beagle, a British ship piloted by Commander Robert Fitz-
Roy, would soon be departing on a five-year voyage to
map and gather scientific information from foreign lands.
FitzRoy was looking for a naturalist for the expedition and
Henslow had personally recommended Darwin. Henslow
wrote:

> I have stated that I consider you to be the best qualified
> person I know of who is likely to undertake such a situa-
> tion. I state this not in the supposition of your being a
> finished naturalist, but as amply qualified for collecting,
> observing and noting anything worthy to be noted in
> Natural History. . . . Captain FitzRoy wants a man (I
> understand) more as a companion than a mere collector,
> and would not take any one, however good a naturalist,

who was not recommended likewise to him as a *gentleman*.

Darwin was overjoyed and immediately prepared to go to London for an interview with Captain FitzRoy. But Dr. Darwin was not as enthusiastic about the venture as was his son. Darwin's father objected to the trip on the grounds that it would interfere with the young man's plans to enter the clergy. The journey would also be uncomfortable, Dr. Darwin declared. And what if Darwin and the ship's captain did not get along? They would be stuck with each other for five long years. In addition, said Darwin's father, such a voyage was bound to be a waste. After all, what use could there be in any information about such distant and primitive lands? Yet Dr. Darwin did not want his son to think

The Hunterian Museum, pictured here, was founded at Glasgow University, Scotland, in 1783, and was celebrated for its zoological and mineral specimens. Darwin studied geology and fossil remains of plant and animal life with Professor Adam Sedgwick, who, along with Henslow, urged Darwin to take field trips to study firsthand the nature of fossils and living things.

he was unreasonable. "If you can find any man of common sense who advises you to go," he said bluntly, "I will give my consent." Darwin immediately turned to his uncle, Josiah Wedgwood, who disagreed with Dr. Darwin. Wedgwood wrote a long, impassioned letter urging the elder Darwin to change his mind. Such an expedition, argued Wedgwood, was a once-in-a-lifetime opportunity and Dr. Darwin, a "most sensible man," should not stand in his son's way. Swayed by Wedgwood's comments, Dr. Darwin consented.

On September 5, 1831, Darwin met with Captain Fitz-Roy in London. Describing their first encounter, biographers L. Sprague De Camp and Catherine Crook De Camp wrote in their book *Darwin and His Great Discovery* (1972):

> He found the captain astonishingly young—twenty-three, only a year older than Darwin himself. FitzRoy was slight but erect, with an eagle beak of a nose. . . . He had been in the navy from the age of fourteen and had already made his mark as a natural leader of men: devoted to his duty, strict, energetic, efficient, competent, determined, fearless, generous, and just. He was even a bit of an artist. . . . Later, FitzRoy confided to Darwin that at first he had been prejudiced against him because of the shape of his nose. He had been reading the theories of Swiss naturalist Lavater, who fancied that men's characters could be judged from their features. . . . Once they began to talk, however, the nose was forgotten.

The two men hit it off and a few days later FitzRoy informed Darwin that he had decided to take him on the voyage. The elated Darwin did not realize at the time just how drastically the pending trip would alter his life. And no one had an inkling that the information gathered on this fateful journey would forever change the course of science and human thought.

Moritz Rugendas's engraving of a Brazilian rain forest ignited Darwin's desire to visit a tropical rain forest. Darwin found the real forests he encountered in South America during his five years of scientific exploration on the Beagle *even more magnificent and majestic than he had imagined.*

3

Voyage into the Unknown

THE 90-FOOT-LONG HMS *Beagle* set sail on its grand voyage of discovery on December 27, 1831. Almost immediately, off the coast of France, the vessel encountered rough seas where huge waves tossed the ship to and fro. Charles Darwin, who had never before been to sea, quickly learned about the miseries of seasickness. For days the only food he could keep down was raisins, and he lay prostrate in his cabin, his stomach seemingly turned upside down. For the young naturalist, the incessant swaying of the ship was made worse by the fact that his cabin was in the stern, or rear, of the boat, the section that pitched the most in the wind and waves.

Furthermore, the cabin, which Darwin shared with the ship's surveyor, was tiny and cramped. It held not only the ship's chart table and Darwin's makeshift laboratory, but also loads of scientific equipment that Captain FitzRoy insisted upon bringing along. An uncomfortable hammock strung above the charts served as Darwin's bed and he could stretch out fully only by extending his feet out into empty space. He wrote to Henslow, "I have just enough room to turn around and that is all."

In all, 74 people sailed aboard the *Beagle*. In addition to Darwin and the captain, there was an official expedition artist, an instrument maker, and a cabin boy, Syms Covington, who was assigned to Darwin as his personal assistant. There were also three Indians, two men and a woman, who had been taken captive on one of the ship's prior voyages. Natives of Tierra del Fuego, the island at the southern tip of South America, they had been taken to England, educated, and outfitted at FitzRoy's own expense. He called the men York Minster and Jemmy Button, and the woman Fuegia Basket, and it was his intention to return them to their own country on the present voyage. Richard Matthews, a Christian missionary who hoped to

A drawing of the 90-foot Beagle, *by Darwin's shipmate Philip Parker King, shows the middle section, fore and aft. Darwin shared a cabin with the ship's surveyor and had to squeeze his laboratory into the tiny room, which also contained the ship's charts and scientific equipment.*

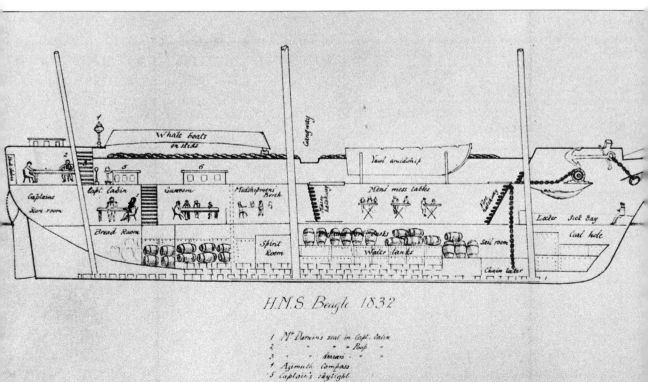

bring religion and "civilized" European ways to the Indians, accompanied them.

Because of his queasy stomach, Darwin was thankful when the ship made a stop on January 16, 1832, in the Cape Verde Islands off the northwestern coast of Africa. The eager young naturalist quickly went ashore and began observing, collecting, and note-taking. He had undergone a dramatic reversal of attitude since his younger, more frivolous student days. Now believing adamantly that it was a sin to waste time, he told his father in one of his first letters home: "A man who dares to waste one hour of time has not discovered the value of life." Even when the ship resumed the journey, Darwin kept himself constantly busy. For instance, he contrived a special net that dragged behind the vessel and scooped up fish and other sea creatures, which he ardently dissected and studied by lamplight at night. FitzRoy, duly impressed, wrote in his diary, "Darwin is a very sensible, hard-working man, and a very pleasant messmate. I never saw a 'shore-going fellow' come into the ways of a ship so thoroughly as Darwin."

When not collecting and examining plants and animals, Darwin spent much of the Atlantic crossing reading. One book he found particularly fascinating was a recently published volume by the eminent geologist Charles Lyell. Titled *The Principles of Geology,* Lyell's book challenged many of the widely held scientific notions of the day.

During the early 1800s, almost all scholars still believed strongly in the biblical explanation for the origins of the different plant and animal species in the world. God, they said, had created all species in their present forms. However, no one could deny that for several decades people had been finding fossils, the remains or impressions in the rocks left behind by ancient plants and animals, in many parts of the world. For example, the fossilized bones of giant lizards, which had at the time only recently been named dinosaurs by the English zoologist Richard Owen, had been discovered in Europe. These were the first

Captain Robert FitzRoy, as drawn by Philip Parker King during the first voyage of the Beagle, *was only a year older than Darwin. FitzRoy and Darwin soon disagreed about the earth's geological history and the progression of life-forms: FitzRoy believed that every word in the Bible was literal fact, whereas Darwin supported Sir Charles Lyell's view that the earth was untold millions of years old.*

examples of creatures that had apparently once existed and then became extinct. To reconcile the idea of extinct species with biblical teachings, most scholars advocated the doctrine known as "catastrophism." According to this theory, God had created many ancient species, and then destroyed them by subjecting the earth to great upheavals. Monumental earthquakes and floods killed and buried the animals, and God then proceeded with a second act of creation. Most who supported this view held that there had been several creations and catastrophes, the last great disaster being Noah's flood as described in the Bible. This thesis seemed to explain neatly how so many extinct species, very different in form from those existing today, came to be and got into the ground.

But Lyell disagreed with the catastrophism doctrine. He insisted that it was not necessary to attribute the massive changes of the earth's surface in the past to worldwide disasters wrought by a vengeful God. According to Lyell, all of the observed physical changes of the mountains, valleys, seacoasts, and so on could have been caused by ordinary natural forces, such as erosion by wind and water, regular earthquakes, and volcanic activity. The one all-important factor, said Lyell, was time. Ordinary forces could easily do the job if given sufficient millions of years. Thus, the thrust of Lyell's argument, and what made his book very controversial in learned circles, was the idea that the earth, along with its progression of life forms, was untold millions of years old.

Darwin carefully considered the idea and already felt himself being won over to this new way of viewing the planet's past. In a series of conversations, he told Captain FitzRoy about what he had been reading. To Darwin's dismay, FitzRoy sternly rejected the idea and criticized the naturalist for even considering such "blasphemy." The captain explained that he believed every word in the Bible was literal fact. Not only that, he had taken Darwin along on the trip with the express purpose of finding evidence to back up the religious explanation for the Creation. Surprised and uncomfortable, Darwin tried to argue the point but FitzRoy's rising anger convinced him to keep his opinions to himself. In the next few years on the voyage, thought Darwin, perhaps he would have the opportunity to put Lyell's theory to the test.

Finally, the *Beagle* made it across the stormy Atlantic Ocean and arrived off the coast of Brazil in South America on February 28, 1832. During an 18-day stay, Darwin explored the lush tropical rain forest that loomed like an impenetrable wall near the coast. In his journal, the excited Darwin wrote how the strangeness of the forest delighted him:

> Delight itself, however, is a weak term to express the feelings of a naturalist who, for the first time, has wandered by himself in a Brazilian forest. The elegance of the grasses, the novelty of the parasitical plants [those that trap and digest insects], the beauty of the flowers, the glossy green of the foliage, but above all the general luxuriance of the vegetation, filled me with admiration. A most paradoxical contrasting mixture of sound and silence pervades the shady parts of the wood. The noise from the insects is so loud, that it may be heard even in a vessel anchored several hundred feet from shore; yet within the recesses of the forest a universal silence appears to reign.

Darwin was sorry to leave the rain forest but found the ship's next stop equally interesting in its own way. On April 4, the vessel sailed into the wide harbor of Rio de Janeiro, Brazil's largest city. Here, in contrast to the preceding stop in a wilder section of the country, Darwin witnessed how a burgeoning human population had already eliminated much of the rain forest along the coast. The trees had been cut down to make way for sprawling collections of huts to house the poor and slaves, huge

(continued on page 42)

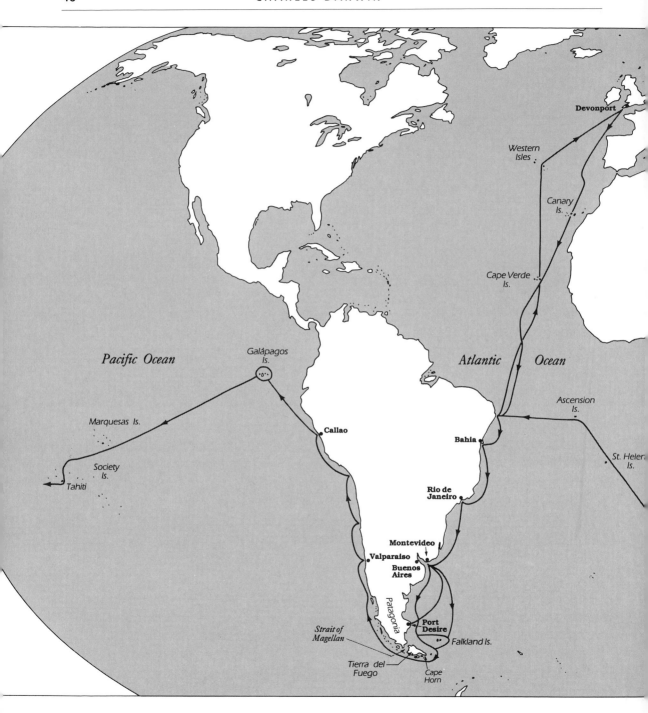

Pacific Ocean

Galápagos
Is.

Marquesas Is.

Society
Is.

Tahiti

Callao

Atlantic Ocean

Devonport

Western
Isles

Canary
Is.

Cape Verde
Is.

Ascension
Is.

Bahia

St. Helena
Is.

Rio de
Janeiro

Montevideo

Valparaiso

Buenos
Aires

Patagonia

Strait of
Magellan

Tierra del
Fuego

Port
Desire

Falkland Is.

Cape
Horn

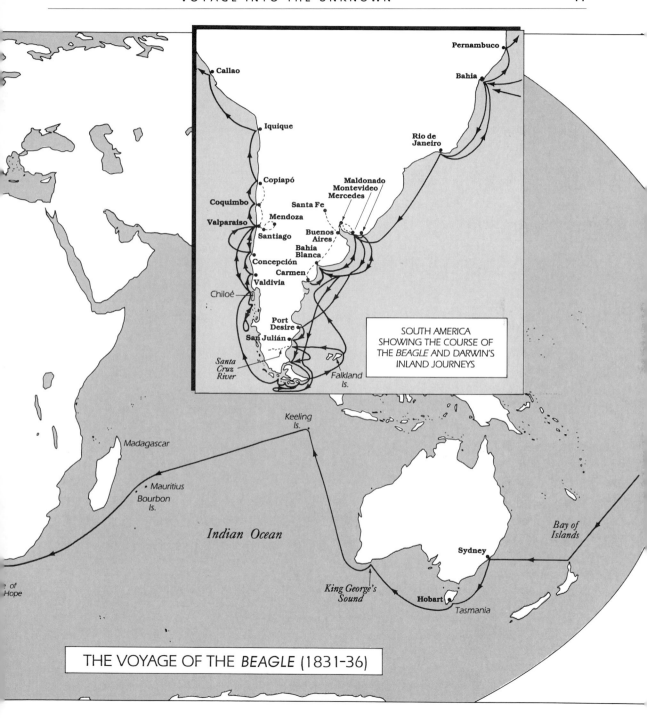

Pernambuco

Bahia

Callao

Rio de
Janeiro

Iquique

Copiapó

Maldonado
Montevideo
Mercedes

Coquimbo

Santa Fe

Valparaiso

Mendoza

Santiago

Buenos
Aires

Bahia
Blanca

Concepción

Carmen

Valdivia

Chiloé

Port
Desire

San Julián

Santa
Cruz
River

Falkland
Is.

SOUTH AMERICA
SHOWING THE COURSE OF
THE *BEAGLE* AND DARWIN'S
INLAND JOURNEYS

Keeling
Is.

Madagascar

Mauritius
Bourbon
Is.

Indian Ocean

*Bay of
Islands*

Sydney

e of
Hope

*King George's
Sound*

Hobart

Tasmania

THE VOYAGE OF THE *BEAGLE* (1831-36)

(continued from page 39)

farms, and immense coffee plantations. Darwin was scheduled for a three-month stay in Rio, during which he hoped to explore the surrounding countryside.

Though he did not intend it, the naturalist got himself into trouble almost immediately after stepping off the boat. He was appalled at the brutal treatment of slaves he observed all around him. Both of Darwin's grandfathers had been staunch abolitionists who had worked politically to eliminate slavery, and Darwin had grown up believing the institution was both unnecessary and evil. Here in Brazil, he learned to his sorrow, the entire economy depended on the cheap labor provided by slaves. Darwin watched in horror one day as a local man he was visiting savagely beat a six-year-old boy with a whip for bringing Darwin a glass of cloudy water. Later, he was trying to take a ferry in Rio and, because he did not speak Portuguese, the language of

On April 4, 1832, the Beagle *sailed into the bustling harbor of Rio de Janeiro, Brazil. Darwin witnessed the brutal treatment of slaves the moment he arrived in Rio and was disgusted by what he saw. He had grown up in an abolitionist family and believed the institution of slavery was both unnecessary and evil.*

the country, he shouted and waved his hands to make the black ferryman understand. Thinking that Darwin was going to strike him, the man dropped his hands, closed his eyes and waited submissively for the expected beating. "I shall never forget my feelings of surprise, disgust, and shame," Darwin later said, "at seeing a great powerful man afraid even to ward off a blow."

When Darwin told Captain FitzRoy about the terrible treatment of slaves he had witnessed, the skipper shrugged and said that slavery was not all that bad. FitzRoy recalled visiting a plantation and watching as the master asked his slaves if they minded working for him. They had all answered no, the captain claimed. Darwin then asked FitzRoy if he was gullible enough to believe that the slaves would answer yes when they would surely be beaten for it. This angered FitzRoy, who began yelling at Darwin. A few

In South America, the crew of the Beagle *made several trips inland to study the countryside and to meet the native peoples. During one of their excursions, Darwin and his fellow explorers came upon a South American native hut built of leaves similar to the ones pictured here.*

days later, the captain formally apologized for his behavior and asked Darwin to forget about it, but both men knew that they would probably never agree on the matter.

After leaving Brazil, the *Beagle* traveled farther down the coast of South America to Argentina. After some brief stops along the banks of the Río de la Plata, the ship sailed another 400 miles down the coast to Bahía Blanca. There Darwin learned that the local people of Spanish descent were waging a war of extermination against the native Indians of the area. This was similar to and even more violent than the battles taking place at the same time between whites and Indians in the United States. Some Argentines told the naturalist that whenever they caught a band of the "barbarian" Indians, they killed everyone older than 20 and kept the younger girls as slaves.

Darwin naturally wanted to avoid this war and spent many of his initial weeks in Argentina exploring a beach known as Punta Alta. At Punta Alta he made a discovery that would later have great bearing on his theories about the evolution of life. On September 23, 1832, he entered in his journal that "to my great joy, I found the head of some large animal stuck in a soft rock. It took me nearly three hours to get it out. As far as I am able to judge, it is allied [related] to the rhinoceros." A few days later, on the same beach, he found some bones belonging to an extinct, 20-foot-tall ground sloth called a megatherium. When Darwin brought the bones aboard ship, FitzRoy remarked that they must be the remains of animals that never made it aboard Noah's ark. But Darwin refused to accept this explanation. Upon examination, what he thought were rhinoceros bones turned out to belong to a toxodon, an extinct, elephant-sized rodent, very similar to the living capybara (an aquatic rodent that looks like a water hog) Darwin had already observed in South America. The main difference between the two species was that the capybaras were only about two feet long. Darwin also remembered seeing small ground sloths in South America that were very similar in their anatomy to the giant megatherium he had found. This was puzzling. Darwin wondered why God would first destroy the ancient rodents and sloths, and then later replace them with almost identical but smaller versions. If the older species had been so corrupt that he felt

The French naturalist Georges Cuvier (1769–1832) coined the name megatherium, *which means "huge beast," to refer to very large animals known only by their fossil remains. Cuvier showed that this skeleton of a sloth discovered in South America was different from that of any living sloth and was therefore the remains of an extinct species. Darwin himself discovered the fossil remains of what he originally thought was a megatherium but later determined to be a toxodon.*

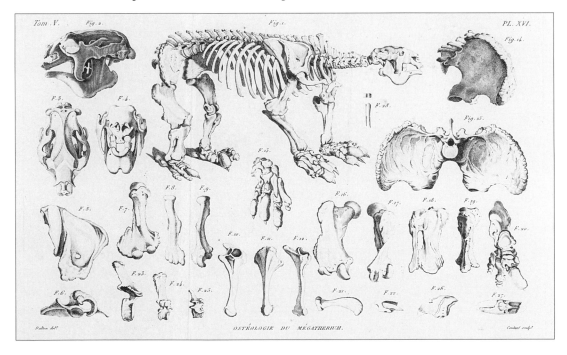

he must destroy them, why did he create them all over again? Could it be that the old and new versions of these species were somehow related? For the time being, Darwin was stumped by this mystery.

He soon discovered another mystery at Punta Alta. It was a living snake with a hardened area on the tip of its tail. When the snake crawled through the grass, it rubbed this tail tip against the grass blades, producing a warning rattling noise similar to that produced by the North American rattlesnake. Here again, Darwin was at a loss to understand the Creator's intentions. If a fully developed rattle worked so well for one species, why give another kind of snake a different, more poorly designed rattle? Could it be that this lowly South American snake had managed to develop its hardened tail all by itself? If so, Darwin realized, it suggested that living species might undergo "improvement," or change, just as his grandfather Erasmus had once suggested.

Eventually, Darwin had to leave the natural treasure trove of Punta Alta behind as the *Beagle* sailed to Tierra del Fuego. At Tierra del Fuego, Darwin became one of a mere handful of Europeans who had met face to face one of the most primitive tribes in the world—the Yaghans. Darwin's fellow travelers, Fuegia Basket, York Minster, and Jemmy Button, were members of this tribe and they had finally returned home. Their relatives greeted them somberly at first, because the three wore European clothes and spoke a strange language. Darwin had the impression that Jemmy and the others might have a difficult time readjusting to their old life. As usual, the naturalist made careful notes about what he observed during the few days the ship stayed at Tierra del Fuego.

After they built a hut for the missionary Richard Matthews, the crew of the ship headed north and returned to the Río de la Plata in Argentina. From there it was a short journey to the mouth of the Río Negro, where, in August 1833, FitzRoy put Darwin ashore. The naturalist now

embarked on a new adventure quite different from the ones he had already experienced. He made an overland trek of more than 500 miles across the rough, sprawling Argentine wilderness known as Patagonia to the growing city of Buenos Aires. Accompanying him were a guide and five gauchos, hardy Argentine cowboys who knew the land and were used to living on the open plains. During the trip, everyone had to sleep on their saddle packs and shoot their own food. Though the journey was rough, Darwin thoroughly enjoyed it and quickly came to admire the gauchos. On his first night with them, he wrote in his journal:

> There is high enjoyment in the independence of the gau-
> cho life—to be able at any moment to pull up your horse,
> and say, "Here we will pass the night." The death-like
> stillness of the plain, the dogs keeping watch, the gipsy-

The Patagonian cavy, which looks like a hare, can move with rabbitlike hops or gallop at speeds of up to 19 miles per hour. Along with his guide and five gauchos, Darwin explored Patagonia, an arid region that includes most of southern Argentina, and marveled at the wildlife he encountered there, including such animals as the cavy and the petises, a rare species of ostrich.

group of Gauchos making their beds around the fire, have left in my mind a strongly-marked picture of this first night, which will never be forgotten.

As the party made its way across the rugged, majestic Patagonian wilderness, Darwin made a number of detailed observations of the mountains, valleys, and other natural formations. He searched in vain for evidence of giant catastrophes in the past. In fact, the more he studied the lay of the land, the more he became convinced that Lyell was right, that the earth's surface had reached its present form gradually over the course of many millions of years. This seemed to rule out the idea of many separate creations.

Darwin made another important observation on his way to Buenos Aires. He had seen the rheas, or South American ostriches, that roamed the northern sections of Argentina. He had also heard the legends about the petises, supposedly a rare species of ostrich found only in Patagonia. Although he doubted its existence, the gauchos repeatedly told him the petises was a real animal. One day the gauchos killed one of the rare ostriches and Darwin was halfway through dinner before he realized what he was eating. Luckily, he managed to save several of the bones for study. Here was another mystery for the young naturalist to ponder. Why would God create two decidedly different species of ostrich and place them so near each other? Could it be that God had indeed created just one kind of ostrich and that, over the course of millions of years, the species had changed, producing descendants that were physically different? Darwin was perplexed and, for the moment, filed this new mystery in the back of his mind with all the others he had encountered on this fantastic journey.

After reaching and spending some time in Buenos Aires, Darwin rejoined the crew of the *Beagle*, and left port at Montevideo. In the following months, the ship sailed back down the coast of the continent and through the Strait of Magellan into the Pacific Ocean. Traveling north, the expedition reached Chile in July 1834. For six weeks,

Darwin explored the mountains of the nearby Andes, and once again could find no evidence of giant catastrophes. All evidence seemed to support Lyell's theory of gradual geologic change. Darwin found further confirmation for this in February 1835, when he lived through a massive earthquake in Valdivia, Chile. Entire villages were destroyed and many people died. Inspecting the devastated areas afterward, Darwin noticed dramatic physical changes in the coastline and foothills. New lakes had been created and rivers had changed their courses. Darwin reasoned that, given enough time, a succession of such ordinary disasters could easily account for the geologic changes apparent in the earth's crust.

Finally, on September 7, 1835, the ship departed South America and arrived in the desolate Galápagos Islands eight days later. Darwin's observations of marked variations in species of finches and giant tortoises from island to island in the archipelago reminded him of the differences between the rheas of northern Argentina and the petises of Patagonia. Many weeks later, as the *Beagle* made its way across the Pacific Ocean toward home, Darwin spent long hours puzzling over these mysteries. He was now convinced beyond any doubt that living species did change over the course of time. The capybaras of South America, he believed, were living descendants of the giant toxodons of ages past. And just one kind of finch, having migrated from the continent to the Galápagos Islands, had somehow given rise to the dozens of varieties now in existence. But how? That was the question that the now veteran naturalist could not answer. He knew that it would take a great deal of time and research to solve this great natural riddle. But no matter how long it might take, he was determined to solve it.

Darwin returned home to England on October 2, 1836, and was told that his appearance had changed during the five years he was away: he looked older, he had gained weight, and he wore wide sideburns. Darwin's father remarked on his son's features, "Why the shape of his head is quite altered!"

4

Birth of the Grand Theory

AFTER COMPLETING ITS HISTORIC five-year scientific expedition and around-the-world voyage, the *Beagle* returned to England on October 2, 1836. Darwin made his way overland to Shrewsbury as quickly as possible. It was so late in the evening of October 4 when he arrived in his hometown that he decided to stay the night in a local inn rather than wake his family. As the De Camps tell it in *Darwin and His Great Discovery*, "The next morning, he walked into the house. He was older and harder than the man who had left home nearly five years before. His lanky form had filled out; heavy sideburns framed his round face. . . . Amid the shrieks of his sisters and the hand-wringing and backclapping of his brother, his stout old father turned to one of his children and said: 'Why, the shape of his head is quite altered!' "

To his surprise, Darwin found that his father no longer expected him to become a minister. In fact, the elder Darwin was tremendously proud of his son's accomplishments. Professor Henslow, Darwin learned, had been circulating the letters the young naturalist had written in faraway lands to scientists and other scholars. Newspapers had printed articles about the voyage for some time and Darwin had become a well-known and respected figure in upper-class society. His relatives urged him to write a book describing his adventures, and he promised to consider the idea.

Darwin's first order of business was to find a place to live and to begin organizing and cataloging the thousands of specimens he had collected. He also looked forward to going through his notebooks and piecing together information about the changes in living species he had observed. Darwin took a room in Cambridge late in 1836 and three months later moved to a small apartment in London. His assistant Syms Covington stayed with him and helped him organize his collections. Darwin decided to take his family's advice. During the next six months, he wrote a 200,000-word volume recounting the adventures of his recent voyage and the book was published under the title

In March 1836, Darwin's assistant, Syms Covington, sketched this view of Albany, Australia, while the Beagle *was anchored in Princess Royal Harbor in King George's Sound. Covington decided to stay with Darwin after they returned to England to help him organize his collections.*

The Journal of Researches into the Geology and Natural History of the Various Countries Visited by H.M.S. "Beagle," under the Command of Captain FitzRoy, R.N., from 1832 to 1836.

During these same months, Darwin met Charles Lyell, whose geology book had given him so many insights during his explorations of South America. Thanks to Henslow, Lyell had actually been following Darwin's exploits and had told Professor Sedgwick on one occasion, "How I long for the return of Darwin!" Darwin and Lyell immediately became fast friends and eagerly traded stories and theories about geology and biology. It was a close and constructive relationship that would last for many decades. Darwin also became acquainted, thanks to an introduction by his brother Erasmus, with the celebrated Scottish historian Thomas Carlyle. At dinner parties given by Lyell and Carlyle, Darwin soon met many other distinguished scholars and authors of the day.

The Scottish geologist Sir Charles Lyell, whose Principles of Geology *had an enormous impact on Darwin, challenged many of the widely-held scientific opinions of the day. He disagreed with the doctrine of catastrophism and taught that the greatest geological changes might have been produced over millions of years by forces still at work, such as erosion by wind and water.*

Soon after finishing his book about the voyage, Darwin finally found the time to sit down and begin organizing his thoughts about evolution. He wrote in his journal, "In July [I] opened [my] first notebook on transmutation [physical change] of species. [I] had been greatly struck from . . . [last] March on [the] character of S. American fossils— and species on Galápagos Archipelago. These facts [are the] origin . . . of all my views." And in his view, the birds and tortoises of the Galápagos, the ostriches and snakes of South America, and all other living things had descended, in each case, from an original and physically different ancestor. Each species on the planet had evolved a little at a time over the course of eons due to some still unexplained process.

Darwin realized that the idea of plants and animals evolving was not a new one. Besides his grandfather, dozens of other scholars had proposed the idea over the years. But none of them could conceive of a convincing explanation for how evolution might happen. As far as most scientists and other scholars were concerned, there was simply no proof for such a process and the idea was discredited in learned circles. Darwin realized that he had to find something new about evolution, something based on the evidence he had found during the *Beagle*'s voyage. But where should he begin? The task of finding such proof and using it to stand up against the entire scientific community was daunting to say the least. One day, in frustration, he picked up one of his notebooks from the voyage and wrote in it, "Scarcely any novelty in my theory . . . only slight differences."

How *were* Darwin's observations and ideas different from those that had preceded him? He spent weeks reviewing past evolutionary theories and seeing how well his own observations fit them. The most renowned ideas concerning evolution were those of French naturalist Jean-Baptiste de Lamarck. In 1809, the year of Darwin's birth, Lamarck had expounded an evolutionary concept he called "transformism." According to this idea, species "low" on nature's scale, that is, those of limited mental and physical abilities, tended to transform gradually into "higher," "more perfect" species. So, said Lamarck, a fish tended toward becoming a reptile, a reptile a mammal, and so forth up nature's ladder.

But Lamarck encountered many pointed criticisms of his theory. For one thing, in the early 1800s, people began to learn a great deal about the physical structure of living things. Scientists such as Frenchman Georges Cuvier, for example, showed that all animals belong to specific groups, called phyla. All of the animals in each phylum have certain unique characteristics that make them very different from any of the animals in other phyla. For instance, all creatures in the phylum arthropoda have segmented bodies and many legs, whereas all creatures in the phylum chordata have backbones. Cuvier and others argued that the differences between phyla are so great that there was no chance of a species changing itself enough to move from one phylum to another.

There were other arguments leveled against Lamarck and other evolutionists. The one that seemed the most logical and obvious to the average person was the fact that no one had ever seen one species changing into another. Lamarck responded that the changes were very small and took hundreds or even thousands of generations to become apparent. Only if a person could live a very long time would he or she notice changes caused by evolution. But people insisted that if evolution was a fact, they should be able to see it happening.

The English clergyman William Paley championed another argument against evolution, one that strongly supported the Bible. Referred to as the "creationist" doctrine, this theory stated that it could not be an accident that each species was perfectly suited to its environment. For years, Darwin himself had noticed that each species seemed to fit a special niche in nature. His favorite example was the woodpecker, which used its specialized beak to forage for insects under tree bark. The bodies of worms, on the other hand, were shaped in just the right way to allow them to tunnel through the ground. According to Paley, such perfect natural designs could not occur because of blind chance or the "mindless strivings" of a species to move up nature's ladder. Paley declared, "The marks of design are too strong to be gotten over. Design must have a designer. That designer must have been a person. That person is God."

Darwin realized that these arguments against evolution sounded very convincing. For his own theory to be worth anything, it had to show how and why one type of creature could undergo random changes and turn into another type of creature that looked exactly like it had been designed on purpose. It was these changes, the thousands of individual adaptations that a species underwent that he needed to explain. "This [is] really perhaps [the] greatest difficulty," he wrote in his journal late in 1837. Later he recalled, "I had always been much struck by such adaptations and until these could be explained it seemed to me almost useless to endeavor to prove by indirect evidence that species have been modified."

It took Darwin 15 months to figure out how plants and animals adapted themselves to their environments and to formulate all of the basic elements of his new and unique evolutionary theory. He approached the problem on a step-by-step basis. In the first step, he examined the relationship between parents and their offspring. Like everyone else, he saw that offspring, including those of animals, resembled their parents. They were not exact replicas of their parents, however. In each succeeding generation, there were always certain small physical differences from the one preceding it. Darwin proposed that such tiny alterations were the basic building blocks that added up over the course of thousands and millions of years to change the form of a species.

But, Darwin realized, it was not quite that simple. His friend Lyell, who did not yet accept the doctrine of evolution, argued that such changes from generation to generation could not end up fundamentally altering a species. A person with a high forehead, for example, might pass that trait on to his or her children. The children might then have higher foreheads. But this process does not continue endlessly, said Lyell, otherwise later generations would have foreheads many feet high. Such changes, he insisted, tended to even out over time. Lyell fell back on creationist thinking, saying that, because a parent woodpecker is perfectly suited to its environment, any of its offspring that are sufficiently different will be *less* suited. A less suited woodpecker, said Lyell, will not fly as well, or peck for insects as well, and therefore its chances for survival will be lower. Nature is harsh, Lyell pointed out, and the offspring that change markedly from the parental norm die off. Lyell called this "the struggle for existence," a process he believed ensured that the perfect forms of species stayed the same.

Darwin knew that, in order to prove the existence of the evolutionary process, he had to find a way around Lyell's argument. Early in 1838, Darwin visited some English cattle breeders and gardeners. It was common knowledge that they routinely bred new variations of cows and plants. They did this by selecting individuals with the desired characteristics, then breeding these together. For example, two cows that gave a little more milk than the average cow could be bred and, after several generations, many of their offspring would also give a little more milk. Darwin thought something similar might be happening in nature. "I soon perceived," he wrote in his journal, "that selection was the keystone of man's success in making useful races of animals and plants. But how selection could be applied to organisms living in the state of nature remained for some time a mystery to me." Most scholars contended that such selection of favored animals and plants was an artificial process invented and imposed by humans. It had nothing to do with what happened in nature, they said.

Consequently, Darwin tried approaching the problem from a different perspective. What about extinction? If Lyell was right, and Darwin was convinced that he was, about geologic and climactic changes happening gradually, then all natural environments slowly changed over the course of time. That meant that animals did not become extinct suddenly in a great catastrophe, but instead died out gradually as their environments changed.

Darwin pondered this idea for weeks and then, quite suddenly, he saw the answer to the entire riddle of evolution. Lyell and the creationists had based their entire argument on the supposition that all living things are perfectly suited to their environments. Darwin now addressed the question of what happens when those environments change. As climate and other environmental factors change, Darwin proposed, the members of a species that were perfectly suited to the old conditions are less suited to the new ones. Of their offspring, some are very much like them and are also less suited. Consequently, their chances of survival are reduced and they tend to die off. If all of the offspring cannot adapt to the new environment, the species becomes extinct. If, however, some of the offspring have changed enough physically so that they can better live in the new environment, they are better suited to it than their parents were. Therefore, they tend to survive and their own offspring tend to do so until the environment changes again.

This process was the exact opposite of Lyell's "struggle for existence" idea. Because he supposed that all species were perfectly suited to their environments, Lyell assumed that nature weeded out the variant, or changed, offspring. Darwin realized that it actually worked the other way around. Nature tended to weed out those offspring that were not variant enough to adapt to changing conditions. Yet, though this idea had the ring of truth, Darwin still could not see how a few changed and better-adapted offspring could account for the gigantic worldwide process of evolution that apparently had taken place.

Darwin worried that too many hours of sustained concentration on the same subject might be clouding his thinking. So, on September 28, 1838, to get his mind off

Darwin studied the diversity of the breeds of fancy pigeons and found the small physical differences of each succeeding generation astonishing. He came to realize that nature tended to weed out those offspring that were not variant enough to adapt to changing environmental conditions.

his work, he sat down to read a book simply for amusement, one he had been meaning to get to for years. It was *An Essay on the Principles of Population* by an English economist and clergyman named Thomas Malthus. To his surprise, Darwin was startled and inspired by what he read. Malthus put forth the theory that populations of people or animals tend to increase geometrically. In other words, if every human couple had four children and each of these had four children of their own, the world's population would double in one generation. At the same rate, the world's population would increase 512 times in just 10 generations. It was Malthus's explanation for why this did not actually happen that interested Darwin. According to Malthus, war, famine, disease, and similar factors tended to kill off many people before they could have children. And because survival was so difficult, the population rose at a much slower rate.

Darwin immediately saw how this idea applied to nature in general. All plants and animals, he realized, were engaged in a savage fight for survival. A single fish laid thousands of eggs and if all of the eggs of every fish hatched and grew to maturity, the ocean would become a solid wall of fish in just a few years. But trillions of fish eggs fail to be fertilized, are destroyed, or are eaten, and only a limited number of fish actually hatch and grow up. Thus, most living things tend to fail. And of the ones that survive, members of the same species are in constant competition for food, water, and warmth. To ensure that its offspring will survive nature's struggle, a parent passes on certain characteristics to its children. Those characteristics that allow the child to adapt to new conditions and survive are the favorable ones. After reading Malthus, Darwin wrote that "it at once struck me that under these circumstances favorable variations would tend to be preserved, and unfavorable ones to be destroyed. The result would be the formation of a new species."

Thus, it appeared to Darwin that nature selects the individuals with favorable characteristics over those with unfavorable ones, just as cattle breeders select the cows who give a little more milk. Because the process he described is a natural one, Darwin called it "natural selection." This, he now realized, must be the driving force behind evolution. "At last I had a theory to work with," he wrote in 1838. But what would be the reaction of the scientific community to this theory? Where was his proof? Would scholars not ridicule him as they had so many other evolutionists? Darwin decided that for the time being it would be best not to publicize his ideas. At the time, he did not realize that many years would pass before he would be ready to share his theory with the world.

Darwin and his eldest son, three-year-old William Erasmus, posed for this daguerreotype in 1842. Darwin and his wife, Emma, had 10 children, 6 of whom were boys.

5

The Silent Years

AFTER DARWIN FORMULATED the basic elements of his evolution theory in 1838, the pace of his life suddenly changed. For many years, while attending college, traveling around the world, and then organizing his notes and specimens, Darwin had been incessantly energetic and busy. Now he settled down to a quieter, more sedentary lifestyle. In the following years, he concentrated on reading, thinking, and collecting the proof needed to back up his new theory. He also began to raise a family and enjoy the pleasures of homelife that he had missed when traveling. Furthermore, his health began to decline and he suffered from chronic illness. All of these factors contributed to his becoming a recluse, a situation that persisted the rest of his life.

Ever since returning from his around-the-world trip, Darwin had been thinking about eventually getting married. He had no particular young woman in mind but recalled the happy homelife of his youth and he knew that the roles of husband and father would be fulfilling for him. On the other hand, he felt that his work as a scientist might be adversely affected by the demands of a wife and family. For a long time, he could not make up his mind about whether or not to seriously consider marriage. Finally, he decided to write down the pros and cons of married life and weigh them against each other.

Thanks to his scientific training, he had become quite systematic and analytical even in nonscientific matters. In one column, labeled "marry," he listed the benefits of marriage, whereas in another column, labeled "not marry," he wrote the drawbacks. Among the benefits he listed were:

> Children—(if it please God)—constant companion, (friend in old age). . . . Home, and someone to take care of house—Charms of music and female chit-chat. . . . My God, it is intolerable to think of spending one's whole life, like a neuter bee, working, working and nothing [to show for it] after all. . . . Imagine living all one's day solitarily in smoky dirty London House.—Only picture to yourself a nice soft wife on a sofa with good fire, and books and music perhaps . . . Marry—Marry—Marry.

Some of the things he put in the "not marry" column were:

> No children, (no second life). . . . Freedom to go where one liked. . . . Conversation of clever men at clubs. Not forced to visit relatives, and to bend in every trifle—to have expense and anxiety of children—perhaps quarrelling. *Loss of time*—cannot read in the evenings—fatness and idleness—anxiety and responsibility—less money for books etc. . . . Perhaps my wife won't like London; then the sentence is banishment and degradation with indolent [lazy] idle fool.

Despite the drawbacks he had listed, Darwin decided marriage was the better choice. On the back of the paper with the columns, he wrote himself this good-natured note: "Never mind my boy—Cheer up—One cannot live this solitary life, with groggy old age, friendless and cold

Darwin's cousin, Emma Wedgwood, was intelligent, worldly, and a talented musician, having studied piano with Frédéric Chopin. After Darwin proposed marriage to Emma in November 1838, she wrote to a friend, "he is the most open, transparent man I ever saw, and every word expresses his real thoughts."

and childless staring one in one's face, already beginning to wrinkle. Never mind, trust to chance—keep a sharp look out [for a perspective bride].—There is many a happy slave."

Though several young ladies in London caught his eye in the spring and summer of 1838, Darwin felt that none of them measured up to his cousin, Emma Wedgwood. The youngest daughter of Josiah Wedgwood and a year older than Darwin, Emma was intelligent, worldly, and a talented musician. For a time, she had studied piano with the world famous virtuoso Frédéric Chopin. Darwin found Emma captivating and finally decided to propose to her in November 1838. Delighted, she accepted immediately, writing in a letter to a friend, "He is the most open, transparent man I ever saw, and every word expresses his real thoughts. He is particularly affectionate and very nice to his father and sisters, and perfectly sweet tempered, and possesses some minor qualities that add particularly to one's happiness—such as being humane to animals."

Darwin and Emma were married on January 29, 1839, and they moved into a rented, furnished house in London. Because of the bright colors of the wallpaper and drapes in the house, Darwin glibly referred to it as "Macaw Cottage," after the bird with brilliant plumage. The Darwins and the Wedgwoods were thrilled about the marriage and both fathers gave the newlyweds large sums of money. Desiring the couple to continue enjoying the benefits of an upper-class lifestyle, Dr. Darwin contributed 500 English pounds a year to the newlyweds. Thus, Darwin and Emma were able to set up housekeeping with the help of a butler, two maids, and a cook.

Partly because they had no financial worries and partly because they enjoyed each other's company so much, Darwin and Emma had what most people considered an ideal marriage. They did not see eye to eye on everything, however. For instance, she enjoyed the theater and he did not. And he was extremely neat whereas she tended to be messy. But they made up for their differences by showing constant affection and respect for each other. Certainly one thing they agreed about was having children. In December 1839, they had their first child, whom they named William, and two years later they had a daughter, Annie. They had 10 children in all, although only 7 of them lived beyond infancy.

Shortly after the wedding, Darwin started feeling ill. At first, he assumed he had something ordinary like the flu, but weeks and then months passed, and he only felt worse. In the grip of the mysterious illness, which plagued him the rest of his life, Darwin suffered from headaches, stomach cramps, sleepless nights, and periodic episodes of extreme fatigue. The doctors who examined him over the years could not identify the problem and none could supply a cure. Doctors in the 20th century have tried to diagnose the disease that Darwin might have had, based on the symptoms described by him and his own physicians. Although it will probably never be confirmed, most modern researchers think Darwin suffered from Chagas' disease, which is an infection found mainly in tropical regions. (It is named after the Brazilian physician Carlos Chagas, who first identified the disease.) The naturalist could easily have contracted the affliction during his field work in South America. Affecting the bloodstream and the heart, Chagas' disease is chronic, or long-lasting, and produces all of the symptoms Darwin displayed.

Emma realized that the noise and fast-paced life of the city was hindering her husband's recovery, so she began looking for a house in the country. In September 1842, they moved into Down House, located in a rural section of Kent, about 16 miles southeast of London. At first, Darwin made

The Darwins moved to Down House in the countryside of Kent, about 16 miles southeast of London, in 1842. Emma had hoped that the seclusion of Down House would help her husband recover from a mysterious illness that caused him to suffer headaches, stomach cramps, and extreme fatigue.

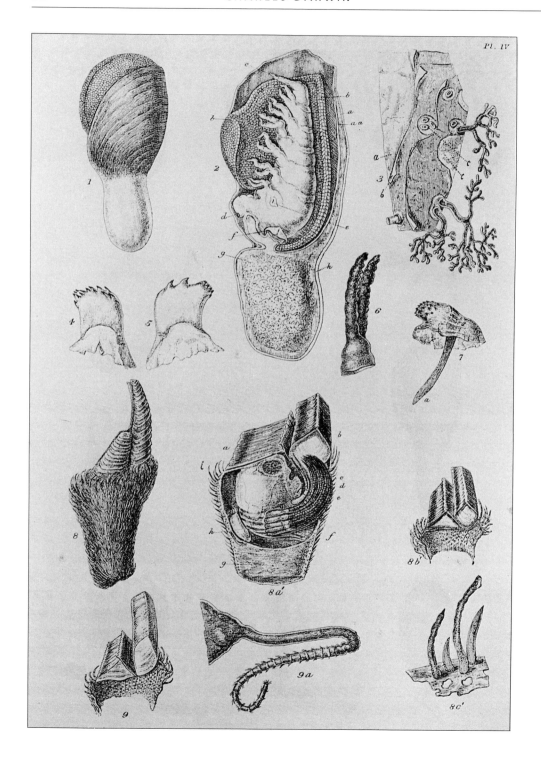

Pl. IV

the two-hour trip into the city to visit friends and colleagues about once a month. But as his fatigue grew worse, he had to end these outings and he retreated into the seclusion of Down House's quiet rooms and gardens. For the rest of Darwin's long life, those who wanted to see him had to travel to Kent.

In the peaceful atmosphere of Down House, Darwin spent much of his time reading and doing research. Almost immediately after moving in, he gathered together the notes about evolution he had made in 1838 and expanded them into a 35-page synopsis of his theory. Over the next two years, he continued to ponder the concept of natural selection, the idea that the members of a species that are best able to adapt to changing conditions are the ones that survive. In 1844, he expanded his notes again, this time writing a 230-page outline in which he explained how several animal and plant species fit the specifications of his theory of evolution.

For a time, Darwin thought about publishing his theory, but once again delayed making his views public. This was partly because he unexpectedly became involved in studying the nature of barnacles. It began with a short paper describing an unusual barnacle he had found off the coast of Chile and quickly grew into an eight-year research project examining every known species of barnacle.

Emma felt that Darwin's preoccupation with barnacles was partly a way of avoiding the publication of his theory of evolution. In his view, he still lacked enough evidence to stand up to the storm of protests and criticisms the creationists would surely level at him. In 1844, a scandal surrounding a best-selling book about evolution that had been published that year intensified Darwin's fear of public condemnation. The book, entitled *Vestiges of the Natural History of Creation* had been written by Robert Chambers. Chambers's theory largely rehashed Lamarck's views, and scholars, including Darwin's friends Lyell and Sedgwick, easily tore apart the author's argu-

Opposite:
These drawings of barnacles are among the countless sketches made by Darwin during his eight years of research on the marine crustaceans. Emma believed that her husband's preoccupation with barnacles was partially a way of evading the publication of his theory of evolution.

ments. The public's reaction to Chambers's book made Darwin uneasy. Many people, scientists, clergy, and the press alike, denounced Chambers. Some said he was trying to "poison" the minds of decent people by going against the religious explanation for creation.

Darwin worried about the negative reactions to his theory so much that he decided to reveal his ideas on evolution to only a few people. One of these was Joseph Hooker, who, in his twenties, was already one of England's leading botanists. Darwin and Hooker had become close friends since Lyell had introduced them in 1839, and Hooker paid frequent visits to Down House all through the 1840s. Much of the information about plants that Darwin needed for his research on evolution came from Hooker. Hooker first learned about this research in a letter in which Darwin confided:

> I have been now ever since my return [from the *Beagle* voyage] engaged in a very presumptuous work, and know no one individual who would not say a very foolish one. . . . I am determined blindly to collect every sort of fact, which could bear in any way on what are species. I have read heaps of agricultural and horticultural books, and have never ceased collecting facts. At last gleams of light have come, and I am almost convinced . . . that species are not (it is like confessing a murder) immutable [unchangeable]. Heaven forfend me from Lamarck's nonsense of a "tendency to progression."

When Darwin showed Hooker the outline he had put together in 1844, Hooker agreed with many of his friend's conclusions. The botanist still expressed doubt about the concept of one species changing into another, but at least showed respect for Darwin's ideas and encouraged him to keep working on the theory. Darwin did keep compiling evidence to support his theory, even though for years his research into barnacles occupied much of his time. One of his many experiments indirectly related to his ideas about evolution involved seeds. To prove his assertion that

The English botanist Joseph Hooker became a close friend of Darwin's after Lyell introduced them to each other in 1839. Hooker frequently visited Darwin at Down House, offered him advice on his theory of evolution, and encouraged Darwin to publish his hypothesis before someone else arrived at the same conclusions.

plants from a continent, such as South America, could make their way to and colonize distant islands, such as the Galápagos, he had to demonstrate that seeds could make such a journey intact. At first, Hooker insisted that no seeds could survive to germinate after floating for long periods in the ocean. Darwin then soaked various kinds of seeds in seawater and planted them. To Hooker's amazement, many did germinate. Darwin also fed seeds to birds to see if the seeds would take root after being expelled in the birds' droppings. In this experiment, he proved conclusively that birds from one landmass could consume seeds and, during migration, transport them to another landmass.

In performing these and other similar experiments, Darwin often had the help of his children. They thoroughly enjoyed roaming the nearby countryside collecting seeds,

Darwin's study—on the right are his stacks of working files and on the left is a curtained privy. His numerous books along the back wall are reflected in the mirror above the mantel. Darwin spent much of his time working in his study; he was such a devoted father that he allowed his children to play there whenever they wanted.

lizard's eggs, and other items for their mild-mannered and good-natured father. Darwin allowed the children to play wherever they wanted—in the woods, the gardens, even in his study. He was so devoted to them, in fact, that he seldom had the heart to scold them. Remembering his disdain for his own father's strictness, he frequently indulged them, and consequently they became fiercely independent and unafraid to voice their feelings to him. On one occasion, Darwin walked into the living room where his young son Leonard was jumping up and down on the sofa. "Oh, Lenny, Lenny," cautioned Darwin, "that's against all rules." The boy's matter-of-fact reply was, "Then I think you had better go out of the room."

By 1854, Darwin had completed his studies of barnacles and many of his experiments relating to evolution. For another two years, he continued to collect information about plants and animals, attempting to make his case for natural selection as strong as possible. Yet, though a full 18 years had passed since he had laid the groundwork for the theory, he was still reluctant to share it with the world. Both Lyell and Hooker still had reservations about evolution. But they recognized that Darwin had amassed a tremendous amount of valuable research and in 1856 they strongly urged him to publish his material. Lyell adamantly told Darwin that he must publish the theory before some other scientist did. Slowly and reluctantly at first, then with increasing momentum and enthusiasm, Darwin began writing the book that soon would shake the foundations of the scientific world.

In 1858, Alfred Russel Wallace, a young naturalist who admired Darwin, sent Darwin a copy of an essay in which he set forth many of the same concepts and arguments on the varieties of species that Darwin himself had been working on for many years. Wallace's letter induced Darwin to step up his writing on The Origin of Species.

6

The Book That Changed the World

IN MAY 1856, with both Lyell and Hooker prodding him to publish his theory of evolution, Charles Darwin began writing a book with the tentative title "Natural Selection." Though two decades had elapsed since he had first conceived his grand theory, Darwin did not feel rushed to complete the project. He worked leisurely at first, convinced that haste would cause him to omit important evidence or arguments. He realized that, in order to stand up to the scrutiny of the scientific community, the book would have to be detailed and cover every aspect of the subject. The volume, he knew, must be a carefully crafted presentation of his decades of observation and deliberation. He must try to anticipate every opposing argument that might later be leveled at him.

Indeed, there were certain key questions about the development of living things that, if not addressed and answered convincingly, would leave gaping holes in his theory. A prime example was the evolution of the eye. The creationists assumed that the eye, a highly specialized organ, had been created in its present form by God. Darwin had to show how the eye could develop in steps over the course of time and such development was, seemingly, very difficult to account for. As biographer Walter Karp explains in *Charles Darwin and the Origin of Species* (1968):

> According to the theory of evolution, there must once have been a time when no animal species had yet evolved an eye that could see. An imperfect eye, a vestige that has only just begun to evolve into an eye, would seem to be totally useless, for what good is an eye that does not permit its owner to see? But if an imperfectly evolved eye is useless, then it will not be preserved by natural selection. Also, it is impossible for it to improve gradually, since a small improvement would not be enough to make it work perfectly—and if it does not work, it is useless and hence the improvement will not be preserved. Therefore, it would seem, the eye is one organ that could not possibly have evolved.

Darwin realized that this and other similar natural riddles would have to be solved before he dared present his theory to the world.

Though they understood that Darwin wanted to be thorough and careful about the presentation of his theory, throughout 1857 Lyell and Hooker continually urged him to work faster. They reminded him that there was no way to tell who might be working on the same theory and, if another scientist published it before he did, Darwin would lose his priority, or claim to being the first to publish the theory. In science, a researcher who registers an invention or publishes an idea before anyone else does is known forever afterward as the originator or discoverer. Lyell commented that it would be a shame if Darwin lost priority for his ideas on evolution after so many years of dedicated work. Darwin did not share his friend's worry, insisting that it was highly unlikely that another scientist was working on the very same idea at the same time.

But he was wrong. On June 18, 1858, a letter arrived at Down House from Alfred Russel Wallace, a young naturalist who was, at that moment, on an expedition to the East Indies. Wallace, who admired Darwin's writings, had written to the older naturalist a few times before. Wallace enclosed a recently-completed essay that he thought Darwin might find interesting. It was titled "On the Tendency of Varieties to Depart Indefinitely from the Original Type." In his letter, Wallace explained:

> In February 1858, I was suffering from a rather severe attack of . . . fever . . . and one day, while lying in my bed . . . the problem [of species undergoing change] again presented itself to me, and led me to think of the . . . [ideas] described by Malthus in his "Essay on Population," a work I had read several years before, and which had made a deep impression on my mind. . . . It is the object of the present paper to show that . . . there is a general principle in nature which will cause many *varieties* to survive the parent species, and to give rise to successive variations departing further and further from the original type. . . . The life of wild animals is a struggle for existence. . . . Now it is clear that . . . those which are best adapted to obtain a regular supply of food, and to defend themselves against the attacks of their enemies . . . must . . . preserve a superiority of population.

After quickly reading Wallace's essay, Darwin was both astounded and upset. Wallace had set forth the very same concepts and arguments that Darwin had been working on for more than 20 years. And like Darwin, Wallace had found inspiration in Malthus's population essay. Unaware of Darwin's work on evolution, the young naturalist asked Darwin for comments, as well as advice on whether to go ahead and publish the article. Darwin realized that if Wallace did publish it, Darwin's claim to priority would be lost. Distressed and unsure of what to do, Darwin hastily wrote to Lyell, admitting: "Your words have come true with a vengeance. . . . I never saw a more striking coincidence; if Wallace had my MS [manuscript] sketch written out in 1842, he could not have made a better short abstract [synopsis]. . . . So all my originality, whatever it may amount to, will be smashed." Darwin also asked Hooker for advice.

Lyell and Hooker acted quickly. They collected Wallace's article and Darwin's 1844 outline and presented them to the Linnean Society, a prestigious scientific organization, on July 17, 1858. Hooker testified that he had read Darwin's outline in the mid-1840s, at least a decade before Wallace had even begun to work on his own theory. The Linnean Society saw to it that both Darwin and Wallace shared credit for the idea but firmly established Darwin's priority. Later, Wallace showed the utmost courtesy, publicly acknowledging that Darwin, whom he considered to be a genius, had been the first to develop the theory of evolution.

Darwin learned his lesson from this incident. To forestall any other possible claimants to his priority, he immediately increased the pace of his writing. During the remainder of 1858 and well into 1859, he worked at a feverish pace, stopping to rest only when forced to by the fatigue brought on by his illness. He completed the manuscript in March 1859 and Lyell's publisher, John Murray, printed it on November 24 of that year under the title, *On the Origin of Species by Means of Natural Selection, or the Preservation of Favoured Races in the Struggle for Life*.

Darwin's book was 500 pages long, some 200,000 words, and very difficult reading. He had not been interested in making his ideas easy to understand for the general reading public. Instead, he aimed his arguments at scientists and scholars, presenting one detailed scientific argument after another to support his thesis. In the text itself

A manuscript page from Darwin's The Origin of Species. *In March 1859, Darwin completed his manuscript, which was published as a 500-page book eight months later. Darwin presented one detailed scientific argument after another to support his theory of evolution—and to counter the criticisms his opponents might later raise.*

he attempted to answer every question and rebut every argument that his opponents might later raise. Many of his colleagues, including Hooker and Wallace, expressed amazement at the breadth and complexity of the book, saying that they themselves could never have compiled such a huge and brilliantly conceived work.

Darwin divided *The Origin of Species* into three sections. In the first, he explained the concept of natural selection and how it works in nature. Characteristics, he wrote, are passed from parents to offspring. But the process is random and always results in small variations from one generation to another. At the same time, said Darwin, life is a struggle for existence in which all species vie for the limited supply of food, water, and space. "Almost invariably," he explained, the struggle "will be most severe between the individuals of the same species, for they frequent the same districts, require the same food, and are exposed to the same dangers."

Darwin's main point was that nature tends to select, or allow the survival of, those individuals whose variations are favorable. In other words, those living entities that manage to adapt to the environmental conditions at hand will survive and pass on their favorable characteristics to their children. The new, favored varieties of plants or animals will, in time, become less and less like their parents. And after thousands of generations have passed, they will have become so different as to constitute a new species.

The second section of Darwin's book was devoted to answering the question: Can the theory be proven false by any known arguments? Acting, in a sense, like one of his opponents, Darwin raised objections to his theory, many of them the most common past criticisms of the idea of evolution. In each case, he overcame the objection with detailed, logical, and persuasive arguments.

One of these objections was the present nonexistence of "transitional" forms of plants and animals. Opponents of evolution had always maintained that, if one species changes slowly into another, there should be living examples of some of the in-between forms of that species. For instance, in addition to elephants, "almost-elephants," that is, creatures that are half elephant and half something else, should also be roaming the plains of Africa. Darwin showed how, in the struggle for existence, the newer forms, which are better adapted for survival, tend to crowd out the older forms. "Thus extinction and natural selection go hand and hand," he wrote. "The parent and all the transitional varieties will generally have been exterminated by the very process of the formation and perfection of the new form."

A second objection commonly raised against evolution dealt with the development of special organs, such as the eye. Darwin admitted that it seemed incredible that an organ as marvelous as the eye of an eagle could result from a long series of random variations. Yet, he pointed out, a careful look at the various kinds of animals known to humanity reveals that they possess very different seeing abilities. Some simple creatures, said Darwin, cannot see at all and only react to light. Some more advanced animals have a simple optic nerve but no eye attached to it. Examining increasingly more complex creatures, Darwin explained, one observes increasingly more complex eyes. Thus, through a series of tiny individual steps occurring over the course of many eons, the highly effective eyes of eagles and humans have developed. Rebutting the creationist argument that God created all life forms separately, Darwin asked the pointed question: Why would God, in His quest to make perfectly suited creatures, create an animal with a primitive, useless optic nerve and no useful eye to go with it?

Another objection Darwin overcame in the book had to do with mammals that live in water, such as whales, dolphins, and otters. According to all available evidence, mammals first developed on land. How, then, could some of them suddenly begin living in the water when they were clearly not adapted to an aquatic environment? Darwin then explained that the change was far from sudden. Animals, he said, tend to go wherever they must to find food. If a land animal finds that fish in a river are its only available food, it will slowly adapt itself to the situation, finding the most effective ways of catching fish. Any physical variations that enable the animal to catch fish

Museum visitors ponder the gigantic skeleton of a whale. One section of Darwin's The Origin of Species *dealt with certain mammals that lived in water, such as whales and dolphins, explaining that they had first developed on land, then had slowly adapted themselves to an aquatic environment in order to more effectively find available food.*

more effectively will make the animal more successful in the struggle for existence. Natural selection, declared Darwin, tends to preserve these favorable variations and the animal may slowly adapt to living in water. He pointed out that a living species of North American polecat, originally strictly a land animal, is equally at home on land and in water. It has developed webbed feet and a special tail to aid in swimming. Other creatures, such as whales, he said, have evolved even further and left the land altogether.

The strongest objection that had been raised previously against the idea of evolution was the argument that there were no transitional forms in the fossil record. According to this view, even if most transitional forms are not alive today, they did exist once, and therefore, people should

have found their remains. When digging for ancient bones, however, scientists had found only the remains of uniquely different species and no transitional forms. To most scholars, the supposed chain of evolution appeared to have missing links. But Darwin held that the fossil record was merely incomplete. The few fossils found to date, he argued, represented only a tiny fraction of one percent of the plants and animals that once lived on the earth. "Only a small portion of the surface of the earth has been geologically explored," he wrote in the book, "and no part with sufficient care, as the important discoveries made every year in Europe prove. No organism wholly soft can be preserved. Shells and bones [often] disappear. . . . Some of the many kinds of animals which live on the beach between high and low water mark seem to be rarely preserved." In time, Darwin believed, more and more remains of transitional forms would be found. Indeed, even as he wrote *The Origin of Species*, scientists were finding species of extinct horses of varying sizes and stages of development. These were clearly more primitive, transitional versions of modern horses.

In the third section of his landmark book, Darwin showed how his theory explained certain facts that previously could not be explained. The fact of extinction had been a mystery and creationists had resorted to theories of catastrophe to explain it. Natural selection solves the mystery, said Darwin. In the struggle for survival, species with favorable characteristics tend to crowd out those that cannot adapt. Extinction is then an inevitable and commonplace occurrence. Darwin also maintained that his theory explained why the most ancient species seen in the fossil record resemble modern ones the least. Because succeeding generations of offspring become less and less like an original set of parents, the longer evolution goes on the less resemblance there is between old and new forms.

Moreover, Darwin's theory explained why certain plants and animals exist in one part of the world and

Darwin pointed out that the North American pole-cat, originally solely a land animal, is equally at home on land and in water, having developed webbed feet and a distinctive tail that aids in swimming. Natural selection, he said, tends to preserve the favorable variations and allow the species to slowly adapt to its changing environment.

not in others. It cannot be, he said, as the creationists maintained—that living things were distributed this way because God had made each species perfectly suited to a specific set of environmental conditions. Conditions in Australia, Southern Africa, and parts of South America are very similar, Darwin pointed out. Yet the animals and plants in these areas are very different. There are no elephants in Australia and no koala bears in Africa. In each area, Darwin stated, when certain species became successful their populations increased, forcing some of their numbers to search for food in neighboring regions. There, they encountered new conditions, adapted to them, and their forms slowly altered to suit their new environments. In this way, over the course of time, each continent evolved its own unique set of flora and fauna.

Relentlessly and convincingly, on page after page, in chapter after chapter, Darwin built his immense case for evolution by natural selection. Near the end of the massive volume, he declared that no false theory could possibly explain so much so well. But would the members of the scientific community see it this way? They certainly knew Darwin was writing a book on evolution, thanks to the presentation of his outline to the Linnean Society the year before. As science writer Isaac Asimov stated in 1960, "The learned world was waiting for the book. Only 1,250 copies were printed and every copy was snapped up on the first day of publication. More copies were printed and they were quickly bought, too. . . . Darwin's book and his theory of evolution by natural selection broke on the world (and not just the scientific world) like a thunderbolt." What followed was one of the greatest controversies and public debates in history.

Biologist and educator Thomas Henry Huxley, seen here lecturing on the gorilla, was a brilliant speaker and popularizer of science for the general public. Huxley was completely won over by Darwin's theory of evolution by natural selection and earned the nickname of "Darwin's bulldog" for his outspoken and fearless defense of his friend.

7

Weathering the Storm

SCHOLARS AND CLERGYMEN ATTACKED *The Origin of Species* ferociously, as Darwin had expected. There were demands for public debates and Darwin knew that his theory would not survive unless it was vigorously defended by someone who understood it and accepted it. But he was not up to the task, either physically or emotionally. His illness had left him frail and he tired easily. Darwin, a very shy and retiring man, a thinker and a writer, had no skills as an orator. The idea of standing before hundreds of people and arguing with experienced public speakers who were out to discredit and destroy him, terrified Darwin. He realized that he must delegate the task of defending the book and theory to someone else, someone he trusted who had credibility in the eyes of the scientific community.

Darwin had three men in mind as his defenders. The first two were his friends Lyell and Hooker. The third was Thomas Henry Huxley, a biologist and educator who had gained notoriety for popularizing science for the masses. A brilliant speaker and debater, Huxley often gave public lectures defending science and opposing orthodox religious explanations on topics such as the age of the earth. Darwin had met Huxley many years before and the two had kept in touch over the years.

Darwin knew that these three men would command attention and respect from scientists, but first he must win them over to his theory of evolution. If he succeeded in doing so, he said, "I should feel that the subject is safe, and all the world might rail [protest], but that ultimately the theory of Natural Selection . . . would prevail." Darwin promptly sent an advance copy of *The Origin of Species* to each of the men.

Hooker delighted in reading the book. He had already accepted the principle of evolution after his many conversations on the subject with Darwin over the years. But the botanist still had some reservations about natural selection, pointing out that there must be additional causes of evolutionary change. Lyell thought the book was a brilliant piece of research but he could not decide whether to accept Darwin's views wholeheartedly. For years, Lyell had been one of the chief voices in the scientific community against the idea of changing species and advocated the religious view of creation. Darwin's theory seemed to make sense, yet he found it difficult to reverse himself so completely on the matter. For the time being, Lyell remained unsure. This was not the case with Huxley. The book thoroughly won him over to evolution by natural selection and he wrote to Darwin:

> No work on Natural History Science has made so great an impression upon me. . . . I trust you will not allow yourself to be in any way disgusted or annoyed by the considerable abuse and misrepresentation which, unless I greatly mistake, is in store for you. . . . As to the curs [scoundrels] which will bark and yelp, you must recollect that some of your friends, at any rate, are endowed with an amount of combativeness which . . . may stand you in good stead. I am sharpening my beak and claws in readiness.

Huxley knew that his friend's ill health, shyness, and mild manners would prevent him from publicly defending his own book. Bold and self-confident, Huxley was not afraid of a public battle over Darwin's theory and took upon himself the task of championing Darwin's ideas. For this, Huxley quickly earned the nickname of "Darwin's bulldog."

The "considerable abuse" that Huxley warned about began to pour in immediately after the book's publication. To Darwin's dismay, one of the first attacks came from his old teacher Adam Sedgwick. In a mean-spirited letter in December 1859, Sedgwick wrote, "I have read your book with more pain than pleasure. Parts of it I admired greatly, parts I laughed at till my sides were almost sore; other parts I read with absolute sorrow, because I think them utterly false and grievously mischievous." According to Sedgwick, Darwin's theory was sure to "sink the human race into a lower grade of degradation than any into which it has fallen since its written record tells us of its history."

Other condemnations soon followed. One clergyman called Darwin "the most dangerous man in England." Richard Owen, the English zoologist and the world's leading authority on dinosaurs and extinct life, was particularly offended by Darwin's book. He had spent his life supporting and defending the religious explanation of the Creation and he feared that public acceptance of Darwin's ideas would endanger the work and reputation he had built. Early in 1860, Owen published a 45-page review of Darwin's book in the highly respected *Edinburgh Review*. Although Owen did not attach his name to the article, everyone, including Darwin, was aware that he was the author. It was a vicious, underhanded, and unfair attack, designed to discredit Darwin in the eyes of people untrained in science. Throughout the article, Owen twisted and misrepresented Darwin's ideas, making it sound as though Darwin was a rank amateur whose work was dismissed by all serious

An overturned statue of Louis Agassiz, a naturalist and zoologist who taught at Harvard University and who accepted the religious doctrine that God had created all living things at one time, exemplifies the topsy-turvy effect Darwin's book had on the scientific and religious community.

scientists. Owen even went so far in the review as to praise his own work above Darwin's.

Louis Agassiz, a Swiss-born naturalist and geologist who taught at Harvard University in Boston, Massachusetts, also became outraged by Darwin's book. Like Owen and many other scholars, Agassiz accepted and taught the doctrine that God had created all living things at one time as described in the Bible. In a lecture to his students he declared that the facts of nature "proclaim aloud that one God, whom man may know, adore, and love; and Natural History must, in good time, become the analysis of the thoughts of the Creator of the Universe, as manifested in the animal and vegetable kingdoms."

Darwin sent Agassiz a copy of *The Origin of Species* and Agassiz reacted predictably. He told fellow scientists in the United States that Darwin's ideas were dangerous because the public might accept them and be swayed into abandoning religion. Agassiz addressed a meeting of the Boston Natural History Society in January 1860 and insisted that Darwin's thesis was "an ingenious but fanciful theory." He added, "The arguments presented by Darwin's book . . . have not made the least impression on my mind."

The avalanche of negative criticism extremely hurt and upset Darwin. Although a few scientists sympathized with him, only a handful went so far as to publicly support him. Darwin found Owen's attack especially insulting. In a letter to Lyell, Darwin wrote that Owen's article "is extremely malignant [spiteful] . . . and I fear will be very damaging . . . it is painful to be hated in the intense degree to which Owen hates me."

Darwin knew that the attacks against him were far from over. He told friends and family he was not looking forward to the annual meeting of the British Association for the Advancement of Science scheduled for June 1860. The major anti-Darwinian forces planned to gather at this prestigious conference and strike a final death blow against *The Origin of Species* and its author. There would be a public debate at the meeting about Darwin's theory and the creationists had chosen as their champion the famous and highly respected bishop of Oxford: Bishop Samuel Wilberforce. Although Wilberforce was an impressive orator, he was very critical of anyone who did not agree with him and his critics referred to him as "Soapy Sam." Owen met with Wilberforce many times before the meeting, coaching him in biology and supplying him with arguments to use against Darwin. In the meantime, Huxley, realizing that Darwin lacked the strength and desire to attend the meeting, prepared to do battle in his friend's stead.

The debate at the meeting on June 28, 1860, at Oxford University ended up being one of the great turning points

Bishop Samuel Wilberforce opposed Huxley in the fierce public debate on Darwin's theory that was held at Oxford University on June 28, 1860. An awe-inspiring orator, Wilberforce confidently championed the creationists' cause, adroitly following the arguments zoologist Richard Owen had carefully prepared for him.

in the history of science. More than 700 people crowded into the university's library, including clergymen, scholars, educators, students, and members of the upper classes—nearly all desiring to see Darwin's theory smashed and discredited. When Bishop Wilberforce entered the hall, the crowd murmured in anticipation. He found Huxley and Hooker waiting for him on the speaker's platform and he flashed them a conceited grin. Darwin's old teacher and friend Henslow opened the meeting and several pre-liminary speakers followed. The crowd, itching to hear Wilberforce demolish Darwin, became increasingly rowdy and eventually shouted at the last speaker to stand down and let the bishop talk.

In this 1871 cartoon, Thomas Nast pokes fun at Charles Darwin (right) and Henry Bergh, the founder of the Society for the Prevention of Cruelty to Animals, who stand before a sobbing gorilla. The gorilla points to Darwin, who is holding The Origin of Species, *and cries to Bergh, "That man wants to claim my pedigree. He says he is one of my descendants." Bergh, to the rescue, replies, "Now, Mr. Darwin, how could you insult him so?"*

Wilberforce saw that the crowd was firmly on his side and confidently began to ridicule Darwin's ideas. Following the arguments Owen had prepared for him, he asked if anyone in the audience had ever seen any plants or animals evolving? Of course not, declared the bishop. All the living things in the world, he said, are the same today as when the Creator first made them. As Wilberforce continued, the audience showed their approval with several bursts of applause. At one point, the bishop asked in a scoffing tone whether any favorable varieties of turnips might tend toward becoming human beings? The crowd laughed and applauded. This was a deliberate distortion of Darwin's views, for he had never proposed that lowly species of one phylum strive to become members of a higher phylum. That was a Lamarckian idea that Darwin himself did not believe. And certainly Darwin did not advocate that plants evolved into animals.

Faithfully following Owen's instructions, Wilberforce continued to denounce evolution, Darwin, and even Huxley, who had not yet spoken. Then the bishop turned to Huxley and rudely asked whether it was through Huxley's grandmother or grandfather that he claimed descent from a monkey? At this, the audience broke into loud applause and cheers, and Wilberforce took his seat.

Now it was Huxley's turn to speak. He briefly rebutted each of the bishop's points, using the logical arguments Darwin had included in his book. Huxley declared that Wilberforce had said nothing new on the subject of evolution and did not even appear to understand the ideas he was denouncing. As to "my personal predilections [preferences] in the matter of ancestry," said Huxley, "if the question is put to me, 'Would I rather have a miserable ape for a grandfather, or a man highly endowed by nature and possessed of great means and influence, and yet who employs these faculties and that influence for the mere purpose of introducing ridicule into a grave scientific discussion'—I unhesitatingly affirm my preference for the ape."

In response to this pointed jab at Bishop Wilberforce, the audience went wild. A few ladies fainted and dozens of students shouted "Mawnkey!" repeatedly at both Wilberforce and Huxley. In the midst of the confusion, a man dashed up onto the platform and held a copy of the Bible above his head. "The Book! The Book!," he screamed, "Human science is nothing!" It was Captain Robert Fitz-Roy of the *Beagle*, who had come to the meeting to testify that he had once warned Darwin not to go against God.

Seeing how a scientific meeting had degenerated into mob rule, Hooker became both angry and disgusted. When the commotion died down, he rose to defend his friend. Though he had once had doubts about natural selection, they seemed to melt away as he approached the podium. The audience sat in stunned silence as Hooker, the foremost botanist in the country, destroyed Wilberforce's arguments one by one. For more than two hours Hooker lectured with passion and conviction, explaining Darwin's views without distortion or ridicule. And then it was over. To everyone's surprise, it was Wilberforce and Owen, not Darwin, who had been discredited.

Darwin was relieved and delighted when he learned the outcome of the meeting. "I would as soon as died as tried to answer the Bishop in such an assembly," he wrote later to Hooker. "Your kindness and affection brought tears to my eyes. . . . I have read so many hostile views that I was beginning to think that perhaps I was wholly in the wrong . . . but now that I hear that you and Huxley will fight publicly . . . I fully believe that our cause will, in the long run, prevail."

And prevail it did. In the following months, there were more debates about Darwin and evolution, and in all these discussions Darwin gained new and influential converts to his views. Huxley and Hooker continued to champion their friend, who, through the verbal and literary storm,

Jokingly, Huxley sketched this illustration of Darwin as pope in a letter he wrote to the hermitlike naturalist in 1868, in which he asked if a German friend could have an audience with him. Huxley's friend hoped to pay "his devotions at the shrine of Mr. Darwin."

remained hermitlike at Down House. So powerful were Darwin's arguments that nearly every important scientist in the world accepted them during the three years following the Oxford debate. In 1863, Darwin's friend Reverend Charles Kingsley wrote to a friend, "Darwin is conquering everywhere and rushing in like a flood, by the mere force of truth and fact." Darwin's book about evolution had ignited a revolution and science would never be the same again.

Darwin took the criticism of his 1871 book The Descent of Man *in stride. When he saw himself depicted as a gorilla in an issue of* Hornet *magazine, Darwin retorted, "the head is cleverly done, but the gorilla is bad; too much chest; it couldn't be like that."*

8

Doing Nothing Just Would Not Do

THE CONTROVERSY SURROUNDING *The Origin of Species* made Darwin a world-renowned figure overnight. Letters from other scientists, as well as from educators, publishers, and many others poured into Down House. As his theory quickly became accepted by the scientific community, the number of distinguished visitors who made the journey to see Darwin in Kent increased. Personally, the great naturalist seemed unaffected by his newfound notoriety. Leaving Huxley and others to travel the world defending evolution, he remained modest, shy, and unassuming, a recluse who rarely ventured out from the comfortable and secure surroundings of his quiet home. Still burdened by his mysterious illness, he became thin and bald, and grew a long white beard, all of which made him look much older than he was. Some of his children joked that he had grown to look like Moses. For the rest of his life, he puttered around the house and gardens, working on the projects that most interested him.

The first project that Darwin tackled after the publication of *The Origin of Species* was, to the surprise of many, not about evolution. Darwin wrote a detailed study about orchids, titled *On the Various Contrivances by Which British and Foreign Orchids are Fertilized by Insects.* The study revealed how these beautiful flowers attract insects and how the insects pick up pollen and transport it to other orchid plants. Darwin became so fascinated by orchids and other flora that he had a greenhouse built on his property. There, he spent many long hours pondering the nature of plants, especially those that climb and capture insects. Because he learned mainly by observation, it was not unusual for him to watch the plants for long intervals, making mental evaluations all the while, a habit that some people did not understand. One day the gardener told a visitor, "Oh, my poor master has been very sadly. I often wish he had something to do. He moons about the garden

Five of Darwin's eight surviving children pose at Down House with his wife, circa 1863 (from left to right): Leonard, Henrietta, Horace, Emma, Elizabeth, Francis, and a visitor. Missing from the photograph are his sons William, George, and Charles.

and I have seen him standing doing nothing before a flower for ten minutes at a time."

Darwin's studies of plants continued through the mid-1860s until he once again decided to address the subject of evolution. Ever since *The Origin of Species* had appeared, nearly all of the public discussions of the book ended up focusing on how human beings fit into the evolutionary scheme. Yet Darwin had said almost nothing specific in his book about the evolution of humans. Many people who accepted Darwin's doctrine automatically concluded that, because humans are animals, they are the end result of millions of years of animal evolution. Others were not so sure, mainly because they refused to believe that humans are animals. Even many of those who readily accepted that plants and animals had evolved clung to the idea that humans are not part of the evolutionary process and had been specially created by God.

Darwin held that it is intelligence, the power of the human brain, that sets *Homo sapiens* apart from other animals. In 1867, Darwin began writing a book entitled *The Descent of Man*, his purpose being to show that even an organ as complex and special as the human brain could be and indeed was produced by the process of natural selection. He intended this volume to be a companion piece for *The Origin of Species*. As he had with the earlier book, Darwin proceeded carefully and logically, one step at a time, building a massive and convincing case that would stand up to the closest examination. In 1869, he suddenly increased the pace of his writing, once more in response to an article by Alfred Wallace. This time, Wallace claimed in print that natural selection could not explain the development of human intelligence. Darwin, surprised and upset, wrote to Wallace. "I hope you have not murdered too completely your own and my child [their idea of natural selection]."

Darwin published *The Descent of Man* in 1871. His main point was not that humans had descended from

Some specimens collected by Darwin appear here on a worktable in his study; just beyond, under a glass jar and next to the window, is his microscope. After his theory of evolution became accepted by the scientific community, Darwin continued to keep busy with his research, turning first to a detailed study of orchids.

modern apes, a popular misconception that still exists today, but instead, that both apes and humans had evolved from some common and less-complex ancestor. If this is true, declared Darwin, then apes and humans should be very similar in structure. And indeed, he argued, the anatomies of apes and humans are astonishingly similar, down to the details of the eyes, inner ears, and even the pores of the skin. If God wanted to make humans special and completely apart from the other animals, Darwin asked, why did he make them almost identical anatomically to apes? Even the brains of humans and apes are nearly the same, Darwin pointed out. Although apes' brains are smaller, he explained, "every chief fissure and fold in the brain of man has its analogy in that of the orang [ape]."

Darwin presented many other facts that supported his thesis. Apes and humans, he indicated, can catch each other's diseases, suggesting that the composition of their blood is very similar. Also, the embryos of apes and humans are nearly identical physically at certain stages of their development. How else can this fact be explained, Darwin asked, except by the theory that apes and humans share a common heredity? Another thing that links the two species, Darwin maintained, is the existence of vestigial, or partially developed, organs in humans. For example, the last few vertebrae in the human spine are structurally similar to the bones in the tails of monkeys. And people also have a small blunt point on the folded edge of the ear, now referred to as "Darwin's point," that corresponds to the point on the upright ears of apes and monkeys. These and other vestigial parts, said Darwin, are leftovers from earlier stages of development that are slowly disappearing or changing as humans continue to evolve.

As far as intelligence itself is concerned, Darwin held that there is no major difference between the kinds of intelligence displayed by apes and humans. Humans are simply *more* intelligent. If one closely observes the behavior of apes, Darwin explained, it becomes obvious that they display curiosity, happiness, sadness, and other emotions. They also have the ability to learn, to remember, and to reason on a rudimentary level. These favorable qualities are all seen, to a more advanced degree, in humans, who obviously have been more successful in nature's struggle than apes. It is perfectly reasonable to infer, Darwin stated, that nature would tend to select such favorable qualities. In other words, early humans developed advanced intelligence because it enabled them to adapt better to their environment, to survive, and to become successful in the struggle for existence.

At the end of the book, Darwin wrote:

> The main conclusion arrived at in this work, namely that man is descended from some lowly organized form, will, I regret to think, be highly distasteful to many. . . . But there can hardly be any doubt that we are descended from barbarians. The astonishment which I felt on first seeing a party of Fuegians on a wild and broken shore will never be forgotten by me. . . . These men were absolutely naked . . . and their expression was wild, startled, and distrustful. They possessed hardly any arts, and like wild animals lived on what they could catch. . . . He who has seen a savage in his native land will not feel much shame to acknowledge that the blood of some more humble creature flows in his veins. . . . We are not here concerned with hopes or fears; only with the truth as far as our reason permits us to discover it; and I have given the evidence to the best of my ability.

Darwin fully expected this book to provoke the same cries of outrage that *The Origin of Species* had. But the storm of protest did not come. More than a decade had passed since he had shared his theory with the world, and natural selection had since come to be accepted in most learned circles. The majority of scientists greeted *The Descent of Man* with enthusiasm, and universities around the world began incorporating Darwin's new arguments into their biology

Darwin, astride old Tommy, takes an excursion in the 1870s. The strange illness that had plagued him for so many years suddenly disappeared; he took long walks daily and continued to publish scientific articles.

courses. Some critical reviews and denouncements of the book appeared in the popular press but this time Darwin took them in his stride. For example, the English magazine *Hornet* printed a cartoon depicting Darwin's head atop the torso of a gorilla. "The head is cleverly done," quipped the naturalist, "but the gorilla is bad; too much chest; it couldn't be like that."

In the following years, though aging and weak, Darwin continued to read, write, and experiment in his greenhouse. "I cannot endure doing nothing," he wrote to a friend, "so I suppose I shall go on as long as I can without obviously making a fool of myself." Far from appearing foolish, Darwin went on writing large scholarly volumes, though none were as momentous and controversial as *The Origin of Species* and its sequel. He published *The Expression of the Emotions of Man and Animals* in 1872, and followed it with *Insectivorous Plants* and *The Movements and Habits of Climbing Plants* in 1875. He completed three more detailed, meticulously researched books about plants between 1876 and 1880.

While working on these projects, Darwin continued to spend a great deal of time with Emma and his children. Most of the children had grown up and left home by the 1870s but they paid frequent visits to Down House. Darwin also happily greeted the many guests who came from all over the world to meet and converse with him. Though Darwin was as shy and unassuming as usual, he had become a legend in his own time, and many first-time visitors were extremely nervous and excited about meeting him. One young researcher was so anxious that when he met Darwin he could not speak and finally burst into tears. Another scientist's excitement was so great that he was awake all night after meeting his idol. Still his modest self, Darwin found such adoration a mystery.

Charles Darwin died on April 19, 1882, at the age of 73, and was buried in England's national shrine, Westminster Abbey, in London.

Opposite:

Charles Darwin's ideas revolutionized biology, zoology, botany, and other sciences by showing that all species did change and that some went on to evolve into more complex forms. The white-bearded recluse of Down House bestowed upon his fellow human beings an extraordinary honor—a glimpse of their true place in nature.

It was during these last years of Darwin's life that he experienced something far more mysterious than being the object of hero worship. The strange illness that had sapped his strength for more than three decades suddenly and inexplicably disappeared. Feeling much better, he continued to turn out scientific articles well past his 70th birthday and took daily walks through the nearby countryside. He especially liked one wooded walkway he had long ago nicknamed his "thinking path."

Although the disease had gone, it had taken its toll on Darwin's heart and arteries. In December 1881, he suffered a heart seizure at a friend's house in London. Another and more serious seizure came a few months later, on April 19, 1882, at Down House. Darwin regained consciousness just long enough to tell Emma, "I am not the least afraid of death. Remember what a good wife you have been to me. Tell all my children to remember how good they have been to me." Darwin died that afternoon at the age of 73. A week later, in a solemn ceremony in Westminster Abbey in London, his coffin was placed near that of Sir Isaac Newton—the mathematician who is best known for his laws of motion and gravity—another great scientist whose ideas had forever changed the world.

Modest to the last, Darwin never sensed the huge legacy he had left his fellow humans. In his brief autobiography, written in his late sixties, he had portrayed himself as a rather ordinary person. "I have no great quickness of apprehension or wit," he wrote, "which is so remarkable in some clever men, for instance, Huxley." He added:

> I am therefore a poor critic. . . . So poor in one sense is my memory, that I have never been able to remember for more than a few days a single date or a line of poetry. . . . My success as a man of science, whatever this may have amounted to, has been determined, as far as I can judge, by . . . [my] love of science—unbounded patience in long reflecting over any subject—industry in observing and collecting facts—and a fair share of invention as well as

of common sense. With such moderate abilities as I possess, it is truly surprising that I should have influenced to a considerable extent the belief of scientific men on some important points.

Darwin's abilities had hardly been moderate. Few men in history have looked out upon the natural world, observed so much, and subsequently drawn such brilliant conclusions. What Darwin's success amounted to was the sudden illumination of the darkness surrounding the origins of life on earth. Although at first many did not want to believe it, Darwin showed conclusively that all species did change and that some went on to evolve into more complex forms.

Darwin also showed that science and religion are not at opposite poles. The fact of evolution did not eliminate the role of the Creator as so many had feared. In fact, Darwin himself remained deeply religious all his life. He believed that a God who could design a process capable of evolving an organ as complex as the human brain out of countless billions of random events was all the more miraculous and awe-inspiring.

In showing how people and their fellow creatures came to be, Darwin paved the way for thousands of future scientists and researchers. His ideas quickly revolutionized the study of biology, zoology, botany, and other sciences, opening up doors to new realms of knowledge. Furthermore, Darwin helped people better understand themselves. Armed with what Huxley described as a "passionate honesty" and "vivid imagination," the white-bearded hermit of Down House bestowed upon his fellow human beings a special gift—a glimpse of their true place in nature.

Further Reading

Asimov, Isaac. *The Wellsprings of Life*. New York: Abelard-Schuman, 1960.

Clark, Ronald W. *The Survival of Charles Darwin: A Biography of a Man and an Idea*. New York: Random House, 1984.

Darwin, Charles. *The Origin of Species*. Modern ed. New York: New American Library, 1958.

———. *Autobiography*. Edited by Nora Barlow. Modern ed. New York: Collins, 1958.

Darwin, Francis, ed. *The Life and Letters of Charles Darwin*. New York: Basic Books, 1939.

De Camp, L. Sprague, and Catherine Crook De Camp. *Darwin and His Great Discovery*. New York: Macmillan, 1972.

Desmond, Adrian, and James Moore. *Darwin*. New York: Warner Books, 1992.

Himmelfarb, Gertrude. *Darwin and the Darwinian Revolution*. New York: Norton, 1959.

Irvine, William. *Apes, Angels, & Victorians: The Story of Darwin, Huxley, and Evolution*. New York: McGraw-Hill, 1955.

Karp, Walter. *Charles Darwin and the Origin of Species*. New York: American Heritage, 1968.

Moorehead, Alan. *Darwin and the Beagle*. New York: Harper & Row, 1969.

Chronology

1809   Born Charles Robert Darwin in Shrewsbury, England, on February 12

1825   Begins studying medicine at Edinburgh University

1831   Receives a degree in theology from Cambridge University; leaves London on December 27 aboard the HMS *Beagle* as the ship's naturalist on an around-the-world voyage

1832   The *Beagle* stops at the Cape Verde Islands in January; reaches Brazil on February 28 and docks at Rio de Janeiro on April 4; Darwin finds the remains of a megatherium and a toxodon on a Brazilian beach

1833   Darwin begins an overland trek through Argentina toward Buenos Aires

1834   The *Beagle* reaches Chile

1835   Darwin lives through a severe earthquake in Chile; the *Beagle* reaches the Galápagos Islands in September, where Darwin makes important observations of finches and tortoises

1836   The *Beagle* returns to London on October 2

1837   Darwin writes *The Journal of Researches into the Geology and Natural History of the Various Countries Visited by H.M.S. "Beagle," under the Command of Captain FitzRoy, R.N., from 1832 to 1836.*

1838   Sets down his basic ideas about evolution

1839   Marries Emma Wedgwood on January 29

1842   The Darwins move into Down House in Kent, England

1844   Darwin writes a 230-page outline of his evolutionary ideas

1856   Begins writing *On the Origin Of Species by Means of Natural Selection, or the Preservation of Favoured Races in the Struggle for Life*

1858   Darwin's priority for the theory of natural selection is established by the Linnean Society

1859   *On the Origin of Species* is finished in March and later published on November 24

1860   Scientist Louis Agassiz publicly denounces Darwin; Darwin's supporters successfully defend his theory in the "Battle of Oxford," a debate at Oxford University

1867   Darwin begins writing *The Descent of Man*

1871   Finishes and publishes *The Descent of Man*

1872   Publishes *The Expression of the Emotions of Man and Animals*

1875   Publishes *The Movements and Habits of Climbing Plants*

1881   Darwin suffers a heart seizure

1882   Suffers a second heart seizure and dies on April 19 at age 73

Index

PICTURE CREDITS

Don Nardo is an actor, filmmaker, composer, and award-winning author. He has written articles, short stories, and more than 35 books, as well as screenplays and teleplays, including work for Warner Brothers and ABC television. He has appeared in dozens of stage productions and has worked in front of or behind the camera in more than 20 films. His musical compositions, such as his oratorio *Richard III*, and his film score for a version of *The Time Machine*, have been played by regional orchestras. Mr. Nardo lives with his wife, Christine, on Cape Cod, Massachusetts.

Vito Perrone is Director of Teacher Education and Chair of Teaching, Curriculum, and Learning Environments at Harvard University. He has previous experience as a public school teacher, a university professor of history, education, and peace studies (University of North Dakota), and as dean of the New School and the Center for Teaching and Learning (both at the University of North Dakota). Dr. Perrone has written extensively about such issues as educational equity, humanities curriculum, progressive education, and evaluation. His most recent books are: *A Letter to Teachers: Reflections on Schooling and the Art of Teaching*; *Enlarging Student Assessment in Schools*; *Working Papers: Reflections on Teachers, Schools, and Communities*; *Visions of Peace*; and *Johanna Knudsen Miller: A Pioneer Teacher*.